DRIVING YOUR INCOME

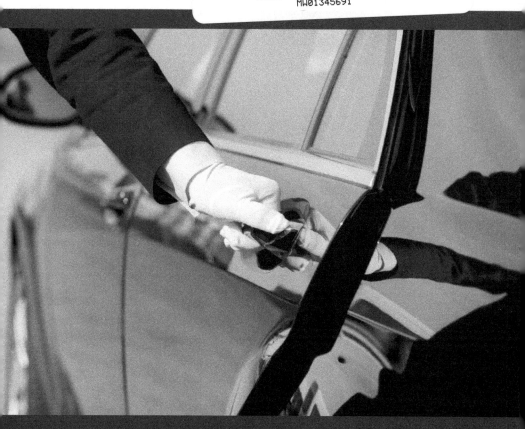

*How to Maximize Your Income
As a Professional Chauffeur*

Kenneth James Lucci

Driving Your Income
How to Maximize Your Income as a Professional Chauffeur
All Rights Reserved.
Copyright © 2018 Kenneth James Lucci
v2.0

The opinions expressed in this manuscript are solely the opinions of the author and do not represent the opinions or thoughts of the publisher. The author has represented and warranted full ownership and/or legal right to publish all the materials in this book.

This book may not be reproduced, transmitted, or stored in whole or in part by any means, including graphic, electronic, or mechanical without the express written consent of the publisher except in the case of brief quotations embodied in critical articles and reviews.

Outskirts Press, Inc.
http://www.outskirtspress.com

ISBN: 978-1-4787-8885-0

Cover Photo © 2018 www.gettyimages.com. All rights reserved - used with permission.

Outskirts Press and the "OP" logo are trademarks belonging to Outskirts Press, Inc.

PRINTED IN THE UNITED STATES OF AMERICA

Foreword

I have known Ken Lucci for over twenty years, first as a customer and then as a friend and business advisor. During that time, I have watched him grow three successful businesses in different industries. He is the consummate entrepreneur and business risk-taker who has consistently displayed wisdom beyond his years. He has a passion for every task he puts his mind to and seeks to be the best at every initiative he undertakes, in true Yankee tradition.

If I were assembling a winning corporate dream team, Ken Lucci would be the top on my list of most valuable players. I would wish him great luck in all his future endeavors, but he seems to do a fine job at making his own.

Henry G (Hank) Steinbrenner III
- General Partner, New York Yankees

Dedicated to the Late and Great Tom Mazza

A true industry icon, advisor, mentor, and best friend

I first met Tom Mazza in 2007 when he became a consultant for Ambassador Limousine. During the first three years of the business he gave me invaluable advice, helped me avoid mistakes, and picked me up after I failed to listen to him and made big mistakes on my own.

He successfully coached me through some of the toughest times in the history of the livery industry, guided me through the acquisition of three limousine companies, and helped my company become a dominant player in our market in short order. If Tom had not passed away in 2012, I am quite sure we would be business partners and coauthors or business partners today. He is primarily responsible for what I have learned and the successes I have enjoyed in the luxury transportation industry. Of all the wisdom he willingly shared, the most valuable lesson he taught me is this:

We are all racing toward the same destination, and our trip could conclude at any time. What matters is not what we have in the end, but what we do each day of the journey, who we befriend, and what memories we build along the way.

Introduction

Why write a book about being a professional chauffeur, and why write it now?

Simple: The luxury transportation business is at a crossroads in its history. Operational challenges, regulatory issues, and new competition are unprecedented, while driverless vehicles are right around the corner.

Never before have consumers had so many transportation options, and never have they demanded more from the companies they buy goods and services from. Never before have our businesses been under such pressures to retain customers, grow revenue, and distinguish ourselves from competitors and industry "disrupters."

Finding and retaining motivated people to properly and consistently deliver the services we provide is a daunting task. We need to do more than just raise the bar on the customer service experience. It is time to break the old bar and erect a new one many times higher than what was once acceptable performance. If this book takes the first step toward that goal with a few people who have a passion for excellence, I have achieved my objective.

OK, I can already hear it now…

> *"So What Makes You Such an Expert on Chauffeured Transportation?"*

My Experience:

- In 2007 started a limousine company called Ambassador Limousine & Sedan Inc. from scratch and reached $1 MILLION in sales in the first 12 months.
- 2009 and 2010, bought the two largest limousine companies in our market and became the largest transportation company on the West Coast of Florida, with 65 vehicles. Achieved new sales of $3.3 million, becoming 5th largest in the state of Florida and #74 largest in the US (LCT Magazine). Combined sales $3.6 million.
- In 2011, the company achieved $4.2 million in sales on our fourth anniversary, which put us among the top 8% of all transportation companies in the US for revenue (LCT).
- In 2012, the company was the primary contracted chauffeured transportation company for both presidential conventions, providing $1.4 million in transportation in 14 days—flawlessly (CNN).
- In 2012, 2013, 2015 the company won Best Transportation Company of Tampa Bay (Tampa Bay Business Journal) in a 100,000-reader voted annual survey.
- In 2013, the company hit $5 million in transportation sales, putting us in the top 5% in the business in terms of revenue nationally (LCT). Sold the company that year to Advantage Limousine, creating the Ambassador Transportation Group.
- Personally executed over 4000 trips, supervised tens of thousands, and trained 500 professional chauffeurs for my companies and several national firms.

About the Author

Kenneth Lucci can best be described as a serial entrepreneur—as in, one of those guys who has grand ideas, starts up businesses, grows the hell out of them, and makes them successful (in some cases). In his 38-year career, he has built four companies from scratch, purchased four other companies who were competitors and made (and spent) many millions of dollars.

He started his first business when he was 15, even before he had a driver's license, when his mother had to drive him to jobs. The company was in the security industry, and he sold it for close to seven figures when he was just 25 and became totally hooked on building businesses. After he sold the first company he built, he went on to become an executive for a large independent corporation and then senior vice president of a Fortune 100 company but soon realized corporate America was no place for him and he preferred being his own boss. At 34, the bug bit him once again, and he started a series of businesses from scratch in the security and medical electronics business that he ultimately grew exponentially, sold to a huge company, and retired at 41.

After a brief hiatus from reality, he started a business in luxury transportation and grew that company to be in the top 50 largest in the US and among top 5% in terms of revenue in the transportation industry. That company, Ambassador Limousine, became nationally known when they performed transportation and security services for companies like the New York Yankees, JP Morgan Chase, and AT&T at the 2012 presidential conventions.

Ken has been featured in a documentary on presidential limousines filmed at the Henry Ford Museum, covered in stories on CNN, countless industry magazines and Ambassador vehicles and staff have been featured on TV nationally during events like the Super Bowl and presidential conventions.

Companies Founded / Positions Held

- Managing Member of HHK Hospitality Group LLC
- Consultant to Ambassador Transportation Group (2014 to Present)
- President, FLEXsedans.com. (2013-14, sold to Tampa Towncar)
- President, Ambassador Limousine & Sedan Inc. (2007-2014- Sold to ATG)
- Business Consultant in the security and transportation industry (2005-2007)
- President & CEO, ResponseLink (1999-2005, sold to Pacific Pulmonary)
- President, Homewatch / Seniorwatch (became ResponseLink bought from Bell South)
- Senior Vice President, Entergy Security, Entergy Utility Co. Inc. (1996-1999)
- Vice President, American Alarm and communications (1992-1996)
- President, Shield Security Systems Inc. (1983-1990 Sold to Alert Centre)

During his security career, Mr. Lucci has designed security and life safety systems, and managed projects and key relationships with corporations and institutions such as Harvard University and The New York Yankees. He has also served as consultant for two product manufacturers, and his contributions have resulted in three patented products. During his transportation career, he founded two luxury transportation companies, purchased three larger competitors, and provided transportation service for companies like AT&T, HP, The New York Yankees, DNC and RNC.

Originally from New England, Mr. Lucci attended Austin Preparatory School, Roger Williams College, and Bentley University. In 2013 Mr. Lucci graduated from the prestigious Ritz-Carlton Executive Leadership Center. He now resides in Massachusetts, Florida and Vermont seasonally.

Table of Contents

Chapter One: What Is a Chauffeur? 1
Chapter Two: Providing a Service 11
Chapter Three: The Qualities of a Professional Chauffeur. 24
Chapter Four: The Four Steps of the Drive. 49
Chapter Five: Knowledge and Communication. 70
Chapter Six: Safe Driving Is Not a Hobby. 84
Chapter Seven: When Something Goes Wrong (and it will!) 100
Chapter Eight: Meet the Passenger 107
Chapter Nine: Special Events 121
Chapter Ten: Celebrities 135
Chapter Eleven: Become an Ambassador of Your Brand 144
Chapter Twelve: Make a Commitment to Yourself,
   Your Passengers and Your Company 159
Epilogue: A Final Word. 165

CHAPTER ONE

What Is a Chauffeur?

> Direct from Merriam Webster's Collegiate Dictionary:
>
> ¹chauf·feur-*noun* \'shō-fər-'\ :a person whose job is to drive people around in a car

This definition is one of the least complete definitions of a word I have ever seen in a dictionary. I have executed thousands of trips personally, dispatched probably a million trips, and trained hundreds of new chauffeurs in my eight years in the Chauffeured Transportation Industry, and professional chauffeurs do much more than drive people around. While our job at its **very** basic level is to transport people from place to place on time every time in comfort and safety, there is much more to being a professional chauffeur in the 21st century than meets the eye. What is more, our job duties are constantly evolving in these changing times.

Today's professional chauffeur is a logician, navigator, concierge, personal assistant, server, stage performer, city tour guide, security agent, and always a trusted confidant. Today our goal is not simply to drive someone around in a car; it is to provide world-class service in an elegant, refined environment, like a luxury hotel suite rolling on wheels.

The Webster's Dictionary definition seems more like the modern definition of a taxi driver and not that of a professional chauffeur. Many novices (both chauffeurs *and* company owners, by the way) who don't know the differences think the two jobs are the same and the duties are interchangeable.

The Difference Between a Professional Chauffeur and a Driver

There is a vast difference between a professional chauffeur and a driver. Just as the Webster's Dictionary does not draw a distinction between being a professional chauffeur and just a "driver," many people make the mistake of thinking the jobs are interchangeable, and they are absolutely not. It is the contention of this book that moving forward, people who choose to become professional chauffeurs must take even greater measures to distinguish themselves from the more common career of "driver" if they wish to be truly successful and maximize their income. The phrase "night and day" comes to mind.

While both drive a vehicle and drive people from place to place, when you think of the word "driver," it is natural to put the word "cab" in front of it and conjure up nightmare rides in dirty cabs in big cities. Conversely, when you think of the word "chauffeur," you may think stretch limousine, expensive, and a guy in a black suit. As competition increases and options in the transportation market diversify, more consumers are becoming exposed to new and innovative types of chauffeured transportation service that are blurring old stereotypes, industry thought processes, and business operational models.

Professional chauffeurs are as different from drivers as a waiter at a five-star restaurant is different from the server at your local Chili's.

What Is a Chauffeur?

The service and amenities provided by a professional chauffeur driving a luxury vehicle should be as different as the Ritz-Carlton is from a La Quinta Inn. While both are lodging establishments that have clean and comfortable rooms, one is a premium luxury brand and the other is a standard hotel. Consumers eating at a five-star restaurant or staying at premium hotel expect much more than consumers who choose a chain restaurant or a bargain hotel brand.

A Brief History of Chauffeuring

Chauffeuring as a task has been around almost since the birth of the automobile itself. The term "chauffeur" is derived from the French term for stoker because the early automobiles were steam-powered, and that meant the driver had to stoke the engine with wood or coal[1]. Early gasoline-powered motorcars, before the advent of electric ignition, were ignited by "hot tubes" in the cylinder head[2]. These had to be pre-heated using a variety of primitive methods before the engine would start. Wealthy owners of motorcars typically did not want to get their hands dirty, so they designated someone to drive and look after these new-fangled machines.

In the early days of automobiles, many vehicles were custom built for the wealthy class who could afford household staff such as butlers and maids. When autos rolled around, someone needed to drive the master or mistress of the house; thus the private driver or chauffeur was born. The chauffeur was also expected to maintain the car, providing maintenance and cleaning, and had to be a skilled mechanic to deal with breakdowns and tire flat tires, which were very common in the earliest years of the automobile.

Since only the very wealthy could afford the first automobiles, they

---

1   Stretching It: The Story of the Limousine, Michael L. Bromley
2   Stretching It: The Story of the Limousine, Michael L. Bromley

generally employed chauffeurs rather than driving themselves. A 1906 article in *The New York Times* reported that ."..the chauffeur problem today is one of the most serious that the automobilist has to deal with," and complained that "...young men of no particular ability, who have been earning from $10 to $12 a week, are suddenly elevated to salaried positions paying from $25 to $50..." and recommended the re-training of existing horse-drawn coach drivers.[3]

Chauffeurs Were Here Before Cabs

The French applied the term "chauffeur" to anyone who was a skilled automobile driver in the late 19th century. Americans decided to use the French term "chauffeur" instead of the English "driver" because in the early days of the automobile, the best cars came from France. In the early 1900s the term "chauffeur" was more flexible; it could mean a wealthy automobile enthusiast, or a privately employed delivery or taxi driver. The term could even refer to anyone who drove an automobile. By the mid 1910s, the term was settled; it was to mean a paid driver-mechanic or just a paid driver.

Taxis and limousines have been around almost as long as there have been automobiles. The first meter-equipped taxi was built in 1897. Cabs first began operating in Paris in 1899, then in London in 1903, and New York in 1907. Cabs charge riders an initial trip fee that includes getting in and the first fraction of a mile and then charge so much a portion of a mile after that. Currently, urban area meter rates are regulated, and rates average $4.50 trip fee and then up to $.80 per ¼ mile. Nationally the average taxi trip is a local trip at about $14.65 in cost and the average urban cab performs just under 19 trips in a 12-hour shift ($245.18 total shift revenue)[4]

---

3   *Stretching It: The Story of the Limousine*, Michael L. Bromley and Tom Mazza
4   Chicago Taxi Report

What Is a Chauffeur?

Taxis use the "metered" method, while livery or limousine services charge by the hour, and as a general rule the more expensive the vehicle and the more passengers it can accommodate, the higher the hourly rate. In the luxury transportation segment of the livery industry, there are also vehicle classes and types that require a multi-hour reservation charter to provide service—like limousines or luxury coaches, for example.

Luxury limousines arrived on the scene not coincidentally about the same time as the taxi cab; however, they were created to serve not the general public but the elite of the early 20th century. The first limousine was built in 1902 and it was designed so the driver sat outside under a covered compartment. The word *limousine* is derived from the name of the French region Limousin because this covered compartment physically resembled the raised hood of the cloak worn by the shepherds there[5].

Limousines have changed greatly since their inception and today fall in to categories many categories from corporate "black car" services whose fleets include luxury sedans and luxury SUVS to limousine-only companies that have specialty stretch limousines used for proms and special occasions.

"Livery" service describes a vehicle and driver for hire that carries passengers and is driven by someone who is a driver by occupation. Vehicles they operate include taxicabs or chauffeured black luxury cars and or limousines, and exclude a rented vehicle driven by the renter.

The Changing Landscape in the Livery Industry

The taxi industry alone is roughly a 11-billion-dollar business and the combined industry known as black car and limousine industry

---

5 Road and Track.com

represents approximately 4 billion dollars a year in total revenue. If you believe what Wall Street writes about the new TNCs app companies, collectively they are reporting to be providing 10 billion dollars in rides each year. So collectively, "for hire" transportation is over a 25-billion-dollar-a-year business and growing.

Driver/ chauffeur employment in the livery transportation industry is projected to grow 16% from 2012 to 2022. This is faster than the average for other occupations in the service sector (forecast at a 12% increase for the same period). This growth will be affected by an increase in traditional taxis, corporate black car services, TNCs, and other new market technology entries and paratransit services due to an aging population.

There are 240,000 taxi drivers in the US and approximately 75,000 cabs, which represents close to an 11-billion-dollar industry standing alone. Taxi services and leasing of medallions to taxi operators represents 78.8% of the entire ground transportation industry today. Unlike the limousine industry, which represents only 7.2% of the total industry, the taxi segment is dominated by large operators that own several hundred cars in their fleets. Most taxis are "leased" by the day or week to drivers. The average cab driver earns a total annual wage of $22,400. There are 13,000 cabs in New York City, alone which equates to almost 20% of the cabs in all of the US[6].

In 2016, the black car and limousine market size was over $4 billion in the United States, which represents only 7.2% of all ground transportation in the US. There were more than 4,000 limousine companies employing 42 thousand workers. The limousine industry is very fragmented business that is permeated by many small *"mom and pop"* operators with an average of less than 12 total vehicles in their fleet. It is estimated that there are 50,000 total limousine vehicles on the road

---

6   New York Taxi and Limousine Commission, 2017

What Is a Chauffeur?

in the US today. There is great disparity in fleet size from the most established large operators to the newest and smallest. In fact, the largest 100 companies in the US have a total of 10,000 vehicles in their fleet, with the remaining 40,000 vehicles spread over the remaining 3900 companies.[7] Unlike taxi cabs, black cars and limousines typically charge for their service by the hour and operators usually require three to five hours minimum service to book a reservation depending upon the capacity and elegance of the vehicle.

New Players: "The Transportation Industry Disruptors"

New players emerged on the livery scene a few years ago and completely "disrupted" the "for hire" transportation industry. Many people say that disruption is far from over. These new "ridesharing" companies have ignored regulations and done substantial damage to the taxi industry and the chauffeured transportation industry in many ways. To their credit, they have streamlined the ordering process and expanded the number of livery passengers substantially.

Collectively and objectively known as Transportation Network Companies, TNCs report that they deliver total ride revenue of about <u>10 BILLION a year</u>, (that's right, almost 2.5X the limousine industry). TNCs, primarily Uber and Lyft, use a smartphone app. to deliver a vehicle on demand to consumers. They have also seemingly let anyone who has a car act as a chauffeur. While it is still difficult to say exactly how much rideshare companies are hurting professional livery companies, this new market entry and livery user demographic is growing exponentially and rider loyalty to these smartphone apps are here to stay.

It is my opinion that anything that increases the number of passengers (guests) using chauffeured transportation exponentially ***can*** be a win for traditional luxury transportation companies and professional

---

[7]   LCT Magazine Fact Book 2016

chauffeurs, but let's save those strategic discussions for another time.

Whether or not the largest TNCs, Lyft and Uber, ultimately make a profit remains to be seen, **but** passengers using apps to electronically call or "hail" vehicles is absolutely 100% here to stay. Whether or not TNCs can make a profit ***and*** adhere to the same regulatory and professional standards as traditional transportation companies remains questionable, and this above everything else will greatly impact their ultimate success and revenue model.

If you already drive for one of the TNCs, you may well be wondering where this leaves you. While I did not write this book for you specifically (still working on that one, so stand by for it), I am very confident you particularly can learn something from reading it. The most important thing I want to convey to you up front is this: *By driving passengers from Point A to Point B and accepting payment, you have (perhaps inadvertently) become part of the long legacy of the chauffeur—so congratulations. Now learn how to really excel at the career.*

If you work for Uber or Lyft and enjoy driving passengers and want to make a real career of it, you must set yourself apart from your fellow TNC drivers to maximize your income competing against other TNC drivers. More importantly, when you find out the income promises made by these TNCs are not based in economic reality (there, I said it!) you may ultimately find yourself wanting to work for mainstream livery companies. You may find the traditional side of chauffeured transportation is more consistent, stable, rewarding, and financially lucrative in the long term. Who knows, but whether you work for a TNC like Uber or a traditional luxury transportation company like those I owned, you are now a chauffeur, and I am confident you will get some good ideas from this book on how to maximize your income while you work in the transportation industry.

What Is a Chauffeur?

Here is a quote I heard from George Steinbrenner, "The Boss," owner of the famed New York Yankees—the winning-est team in the history of professional baseball. It is appropriate for the beginning of this book:

> *"If you are not going to wake up every morning and strive to be the best at what you do, why even get out of bed?"*

Things to Master from Chapter One:

- A driver is concerned about getting you from point A to point B.
- A professional chauffeur is concerned about safe driving *AND Providing the Best Experience along the way.*
- There is a HUGE difference between a driver and a professional chauffeur in all aspects of the job, especially the income.
- You are now part of the exceptional lineage of chauffeurs who have served the wealthy and elite for well over 100 years. Congratulations--ACT ACCORDINGLY.
- A professional chauffeur provides world-class service and involves a myriad of positions all rolled in to one:

    Logician

    Concierge

    Personal Assistant

    City Tour Guide

    Trusted Confidant

- Distinguishing yourself from drivers and learning all the skills of being a professional chauffeur means more rides, more income, and more tips.

- There are and will continue to be new entries into the luxury transportation industry, so you must improve your performance to continually improve your income.

CHAPTER TWO

Providing a Service

> *"A service is a set of one time consumable and perishable benefits"* – Economic definition

When you think of providing a service, think of the service transaction as a performance, an act or better yet, "an experience." The location of the service delivery is referred to as the stage, and the people that facilitate the service process are called the performers. A script is a sequence of behaviors followed by all those involved, including the client(s). Some service experiences are tightly scripted; others are looser or ad lib. The service in the chauffeured transportation industry should be tightly scripted, based on the time-sensitive nature of travel.

Further, the service experiences that are often repeated or ordered frequently by consumers should be very tightly scripted and choreographed because consumers are more likely to judge the service against similar experiences that they have purchased before.

Since the late 1990s, services have become an increasingly important part of the US economy. Service-producing industries accounted for over

80% of total US employment, with some 179,733,700 employees engaged in some kind of service work[8] --and these numbers continue to rise.

The Bureau of Labor Statistics (BLS) defines the service sector to include all industries except those in the goods-producing sector like agriculture, mining, construction, and manufacturing. The service sector, or "service-providing industry," encompasses the industries of wholesale and retail trade, utilities, transportation, information, financial and business activities, professional and technical services, education, health care and social assistance, leisure and hospitality, and miscellaneous services[9].

Many careers are considered part of the service sector, such as accountants, sales reps, architects, engineers, social workers, lawyers, teachers, artists, athletes, reporters, dentists, nurses, electricians, mechanics, airplane pilots, chefs, firefighters, groundskeepers, truck drivers, cab drivers, chauffeurs, and soldiers.

According to the Bureau of Labor Statistics, the service sector of the economy will be the main source of employment and output between now and 2023. Employment in the service sector will increase over 12 percent between now and 2023, while employment in the goods-producing sector is not expected to increase. Overall, economy-wide employment is expected to increase by 10 percent[10].

According to the BLS, employment growth in the Chauffeured Transportation Industry will increase by 16% over the next ten years, which is twice that of other service related industries and three times more of an increase than employment in manufacturing and agriculture.

Choosing to be a professional chauffeur can be financially rewarding, enjoyable, and a long-lasting career for those who master the important service elements of their position.

8	Department of Labor Statistics 2012
9	Bureau of Labor and Statistics, ALFCIO.org
10	Bureau of Labor and Statistics, ALFCIO.org

The delivery of any service typically involves six factors:

- The service provider and facilitators (e.g. the company and their people)
- Equipment used to provide the service (e.g. phones, vehicles, computers)
- The physical facilities (buildings, garage)
- The consumer requesting service (customer)
- Other customers who use the service (who talk good or bad about it)
- **Customer contact at the point of service delivery (THAT WOULD BE YOU!!)**

Examples of Legendary Service

Throughout business world, there are brands in many sectors that stand out as having excellent reputations, with names that are synonymous with service excellence. There is one commonality among these brands: they are all totally focused on the customer service experience. They don't just hang up posters or have slogans; every minute of the day, everything they do is totally focused on achieving 100% customer satisfaction.

They are known as the undisputed leader in their category and the best at what they do. While they may seemingly provide typical products or services, they do it in a way that makes them stand out above fierce competition. They succeed by differentiating themselves from the pack by focusing on providing truly exceptional service.

The Ritz-Carlton Hotels

When I founded my first transportation company, Ambassador Limousine and Sedan Inc. in 2007, I spent a lot of time planning and defining what I wanted our brand to stand for and how we wanted our chauffeurs and other employees to act when dealing with our customers. In short, how did we want to be perceived by the public, our competition, our employees—and most importantly, our customers?

We studied many other industries and we decided that the limousine industry was very akin to the hospitality and hotel industry. I actually studied several hotel businesses and the entrepreneurs who founded them. I read books about Hilton and Marriott and even Leona Helmsley. We dissected and studied the business models of all their companies and "borrowed" operating and service elements from each one and tailored them for the livery industry. In the end we decided to build our branding image similar to the Ritz-Carlton in many ways. Their slogan or business motto is

> *"We Are Ladies and Gentlemen Serving Ladies and Gentlemen"*

The Ritz-Carlton in fact has an Executive Leadership Center that teaches all the elements of their service system. I attended in 2012 and found so many similarities to the livery industry we ended up rewriting our employee manual and training manuals to improve our service and operational system to emulate the Ritz-Carlton even closer than before. I cannot recommend their program enough; it was for me literally a business-changing experience.

At my company Ambassador Limousine and Sedan, we developed many branding elements among them our statement of core values and our slogan that stated with clarity who we were and what our job was:

> *"We Are in the Service of Others with
> Pleasure and Professionalism"*

This slogan served as the basis of our service philosophy and defined for our chauffeurs what our goals were.

While there are many premium hotel brands, no name is more synonymous with luxury, elegance, and a superb experience than the Ritz-Carlton. The name has made it into our vocabulary, meaning to display your best: "Putting on the Ritz."

The legacy of The Ritz-Carlton begins in the 19th century in France with the celebrated hotelier Cesar Ritz, the "king of hoteliers and hotelier to kings" who owned the original Ritz in Paris. His philosophy of service and continued innovation redefined the luxury hotel experience in Europe through his management of The Ritz Paris and The Carlton in London[11].

The Ritz-Carlton revolutionized hospitality by creating luxury in a hotel setting:

- Private bath in each guest room
- Light fabrics in the guest room to allow for more thorough washing
- Impeccably dressed staff featuring White tie and apron uniforms, black tie for the Maître d' and morning suits for all other hotel staff exuding a formal appearance
- Fresh flower displays throughout the public areas
- A la carte dining, providing vast choices for diners
- Gourmet cuisine, utilizing the genius and cooking methods of Auguste Escoffier

---

11   Ritz-Carlton.com

- Intimate, smaller lobbies for a more personalized guest experience

When Cesar Ritz died in 1918, his wife Marie continued the expansion of hotels in Europe bearing his name when the brand came to the attention of an American entrepreneur traveling in France by the name of Albert Keller[11].

Mr. Keller was so impressed he established The Ritz-Carlton Investing Company in the US and bought and franchised the Ritz name and operating system. In 1927 The Ritz-Carlton Boston opened, and other hotels followed in New York, Philadelphia, Pittsburgh, Atlantic City, and Boca Raton[11].

In 1983, The Ritz-Carlton Hotel Company, LLC was formed. Led by president and founding father, Colgate Holmes, alongside Horst Schulze, Joe Freni, Ed Staros, and Herve Humler, the company began to expand, adding new properties across the United States. Within two years, the brand had opened five more hotels. Through the '80s the rapid expansion continued, and by the close of 1992, The Ritz-Carlton had expanded to 23 exceptional luxury hotels[11].

In 1998, the success of The Ritz-Carlton Hotel Company had attracted the attention of the entire hospitality industry, and the brand was purchased by Marriott International. Since this purchase, The Ritz-Carlton has continued to grow, providing exceptional service and genuine care to their guests across the globe. The company now has dozens of new hotels around the globe.

The success of the Ritz-Carlton Hotels has much less to do with the actual hotel buildings or physical amenities and much more to do with their award- winning operating system and comprehensive employee (associate) training processes that are totally focused on guest satisfaction. At the Ritz-Carlton, each new employee is "on boarded" through a unique training process that imparts the Ritz-Carlton culture and values. These values are reinforced daily through the operating system at every hotel and every employee receives more than 100 hours of customer service training annually. Each employee is the customer service department and is empowered to break away from his or her routine duties to assist a guest and is empowered to spend up to $1000 per guest per day to make sure guests are not just satisfied but WOWED. Here is a legendary story from Ritz-Carlton that explains:

> *A businessman was a guest at the hotel with a repeat group who had stayed at the hotel only once before—one year prior for the same conference. When the guest was at the hotel a year ago, he was having dinner in one of the ballrooms and asked a banquet server if it was possible to get his favorite soda beverage. The server informed him that the hotel did not serve that beverage, but he would see what he could do.*
>
> *Within a few moments, the server came back with the requested beverage. And every night for the rest of the conference when they were having dinner, the server had the favorite drink waiting for this guest.*
>
> *Already amazed by the past experience, the guest never expected what happened at the conference the next year. He was sitting in one of the ballrooms having dinner, and in walked his same server from the year before with the beverage in hand. The server completely shocked and delighted the guest by remembering his favorite beverage, even after a year's time[12].*

Consistency, exceptional service, and WOW stories such as these are just a few of the reasons why The Ritz-Carlton was named the two-time winner of the Malcolm Baldridge National Quality Award by the USS Department of Commerce.

---

12   Ritz-Carlton.com

> "We Are Ladies and Gentlemen Serving Ladies and Gentlemen" - Ritz-Carlton Motto

Nordstrom Department Stores

Ask anyone who has ever worked in retail what the first words are that come to their mind when they think of Nordstrom, and they will say "impeccable customer service."

Making your brand synonymous with this important phrase does not happen overnight. In fact, it has taken Nordstrom 115 years of complete focus on creating the finest shopping experience to earn this reputation. There is one legendary story from Nordstrom that perfectly illustrates their service philosophy:

> *A man walked into the Fairbanks, Alaska, Nordstrom department store with two snow tires under his arms. He walked up to the counter, put the tires down and asked for his money back. The clerk, who'd been working there for just two weeks, saw the price tags still on the side of the tires, reached into the cash register and handed the man $145. The customer smiled, the clerk thanked him for his business and both men went on their way.*
>
> *The point of the story—Nordstrom does not sell snow tires, never has.*
>
> *The customer wanted to return the tires. It did not matter that Nordstrom did not sell tires and never sold tires. They sell upscale clothing. The clerk accepted the return simply because that is what the customer wanted and that is what it took to make the customer happy"*[13]

---

13   Utires.com / Nordstrom

So, you may ask, how could that employee do that? It's simple, really; he was trained to use his best judgment to make sure every customer left Nordstrom happy. The clerk saw taking the tires back as his best way to achieve that objective.

At Nordstrom, they keep things very simple. They have one goal: *Make every customer happy and make sure they feel good when they leave*[14]. They work hard every day with this goal in mind. Their entire philosophy revolves around empowering their employees to do whatever it takes to achieve this goal. From their employee manual:

> ***Nordstrom Rules: Rule #1: Use best judgment in all situations***[15]***. There will be no additional rules!***

While other big-name retailers fell on hard times during the most recent recession, Nordstrom continues to grow revenues and profits following a simple formula that starts and ends with being obsessed with superb customer service. Nordstrom has seen a 76% increase in revenue from 2005 to 2014 while maintaining a steady gross profit margin[16].

NORDSTROM	2010	2011	2012	2013	2014	2015	2016	2017
REVENUE USD MIL	8,627	9,700	10,877	12,148	12,540	14,100	14,500	15,100
GROSS MARGIN %	38.2	39.2	39.4	38.8	39.1	36.1	34.9	34.7

---

14   Shopify.com / Nordstrom
15   Shopify.com / Nordstrom
16   Morningstar / Nordstrom

ZAPPOS.com (was a legend in the making, now part of Amazon).

In 1999, Zappos founder Nick Swinmurn went to a local mall in San Francisco to buy a pair of shoes. While one store had the right style, they did not have the right color. Yet another store had the right color, but not in his size. It is reported that Nick spent the rest of the day going from store to store only to go home without shoes and very frustrated[17].

At home Nick looked for his shoes online and was again disappointed. Although there were a lot of retail stores selling shoes online, what was interesting to Nick was that there was no major online retailer that specialized in all things shoes. It was on that day that the idea of Zappos.com was born!

The original idea was to build a website that offered the best selection in shoes anywhere. The goal was to have the most brands, styles, colors, sizes, and widths available all in one place. Over the next nine years, the Zappos brand and what it has become known for have greatly evolved. In addition to offering the best footwear selections, the company has become obsessed with providing the absolute best service available online—not just in the shoes, but in any retail category.

Nick's initial business assumptions and vision when he started were simple[18]:

a) One day, 30% of all retail transactions in the US will be online.

b) People will buy from the company with the best service and the best product selection.

c) Zappos.com will be that online store.

The company believes that the speed at which a customer receives an online purchase plays an extremely important role in how that

---

17   About Zappos.com
18   About Zappos.com

customer thinks about shopping online then and in the future. So Zappos focuses on making sure the items get delivered to customers as quickly as possible. To do that, they physically warehouse everything they sell in every size, width, and color available. Unlike other online retailers, they do not make an item available for sale unless it is physically present in their warehouse.

But speed of delivery is only part of the Zappos story of rapid growth and success. The company now has 500 employees in a call center in Las Vegas who all receive a full seven weeks of training on how to make customers not just happy but ecstatic.

The company (now a unit of Amazon) has been described by many adjectives, including "obsessed," "insane," and "fanatical" for the way it will do anything to please its customers. The stories have quickly become legendary, and are a key part of its brand image and spectacular growth:[19]

- Zappos sent flowers to a woman who ordered six different pairs of shoes because her feet were damaged by harsh medical treatments.
- A customer service rep physically went to a rival shoe store to get a specific pair of shoes for a woman staying at the Mandalay Bay hotel in Vegas when Zappos ran out of stock.
- The same year, it sent a free pair of shoes overnight to a best man who had arrived a wedding shoeless.

Why share stories about these particular businesses in a book on how to be a professional chauffeur?

Simple. These three companies provide seemingly mundane services and products: a comfortable hotel room, clothing, and shoes.

---
[19] BusinessInsider.com

But they became outstanding leaders in their fields because they turn consumers into raving fans by providing exceptional customer service experiences. They have taken ordinary goods and services and created ways to impact the customer experience so positively that they are preferred over their competitors and have extreme customer loyalty. In this book we hope to teach you how as a professional chauffeur you can provide exceptional customer service and maximize your income above and beyond others in your field.

These are just three examples of companies that sell commodities that have risen well above their competition by being fanatics about customer service. We sell a commodity also, and I would like to emphasize to you again that we are NOT in the transportation business, our product is NOT the vehicle and not the ride—we are in the customer service business, and our product is **THE SERVICE EXPERIENCE** we provide before, during, and after the ride.

People forget consumer transactions.

They remember and talk about service experiences.

So, what does it take to turn a very mundane customer service transaction (a ride in a luxury vehicle) into an exceptional customer service experience?

If you said the vehicle you answered incorrectly. You will discover the real answer in the next chapters.

Things to Master from Chapter Two:

- We are in a customer service business with many options for the consumers to choose from. They don't have to choose us!
- We must consistently improve our performance to increase our income.

- The best service providers differentiate the service they provide from competitors.
- They focus on the "experience," not just the basic delivery of the service.
- They go out of their way to WOW the customers every time there is a service interaction.
- In the luxury transportation business:

> *"IT'S NOT JUST ABOUT THE RIDE—
> IT'S ABOUT THE EXPERIENCE!"*

CHAPTER THREE

The Qualities of a Professional Chauffeur

When I interview candidates for chauffeur positions, I ask two initial questions to determine if they possess the characteristics and traits that make up Service DNA:

What is your primary motivation for wanting to become a chauffeur?

Do you think this job is easy?

The answers to these questions determine whether the interview continues.

Let's take the first one: "What is your primary motivation for wanting to be a chauffeur?" If the candidate mentions money in the first sentence, they are typically wrong for the job. Becoming a top earner as a professional chauffeur takes effort, and these candidates are not usually willing to make an effort.

If the answer is something like, "Well, I was recently laid off from…" they are wrong for the job. Someone who was just laid off from a full-time job outside the transportation industry typically thinks they can become a chauffeur until they find something else.

The best candidates tell me that they enjoy interacting with people. They like the hospitality business and service economy, being out and about in the community, and challenges. They don't like being stuck inside an office. They know if they provide quality service, the rewards will be there.

When I ask candidates if they think being a chauffeur is easy, candidates who respond "Yes" are likely to quit even if I hire them. Being a professional chauffeur is not easy. Yes, in most states getting a chauffeur license is a joke; all you have to do is take a quick written test and pay a small fee. But after traveling all over the United States for 30 years, I have observed that less than 30% of chauffeurs *provide exceptional service*. Not that 70% of the rides were horrible; they weren't. They just weren't memorable. Those 70% made no real impression on me as a customer. They failed to create any real customer loyalty; they were just rides. Therefore, I did not use those companies again or recommend them to others.

Service DNA

The best chauffeurs I employed, trained, and observed all over the US over my 8+ years in the livery industry and 20+ years as a customer of chauffeured transportation all share certain traits that combine to exemplify "service DNA."

When I was looking for new chauffeurs or training existing ones, my first two questions were the same and helped me figure out whether the candidate has these traits. I call these characteristics "service DNA."

Service DNA determines your ability—**and more importantly, your desire**—to take care of others. It does not just motivate you to perform seemingly menial tasks for others; it allows you to feel true fulfillment while doing these tasks. At this point I need to state emphatically that I have never seen service DNA faked convincingly. The late comedian George Burns once said, "Sincerity—if you can fake that, you've got it made." Neither sincerity nor service DNA can be faked for long, in my view.

Service DNA is not something you can merely declare you have. It is demonstrated in the way you live. If people describe you as warm, kind, caring, giving, and sincere, or you are frequently described as a "people person," you most likely have it. Conversely, if you are standoffish, shy, aloof, stuck-up, arrogant, or even introverted, you might not have service DNA. That is perfectly fine; some of the brightest and most successful people don't have service DNA. All it means is that the service economy is not for you.

**Service DNA is made up of five A's:
Appearance, Accuracy, Alertness, Attitude, and Anticipation.**

Appearance

In the Peanuts cartoons, a character named "Pig Pen" literally has a cloud of dust and dirt around him as he moves. Pig Pen would not be a good professional chauffeur. Being a professional chauffeur means always looking the part. Whether, rain, snow, or sunshine, the professional chauffeur's vehicle–and the professional chauffeur–looks crisp, clean, and well groomed.

1) Your Personal Appearance

A professional chauffeur looks like a plain-clothes military person, protective agent, professional sales person, or business executive. Looking the part is half the battle.

Cleanliness

If you have tattoos, cover them. If you have visible piercings, take them out before you go to work. If you wear political buttons, leave them home. If you smoke, stop, or at least don't smoke while on duty. Don't smell like you smoke; people who don't smoke get very offended by the smell of smoke. They may not say it to you directly, but they will more than likely take offense.

A male professional chauffeur gets his hair cut every two to three weeks whether it needs it or not. Female professional chauffeurs may not need monthly haircuts, but they should keep their hair neat. Since chauffeuring is a physical job that involves lifting luggage, women may want to keep long hair tied back.

Clothes

Choosing the proper attire for your career as a professional chauffeur is as critical to your success as driving a vehicle that starts reliably. Not only does your wardrobe have to look good; it has to be comfortable and durable, because you will be wearing it a lot and in active situations.

The uniform of the professional chauffeur is typically a black suit, white shirt, and black tie. If you are a formal professional chauffeur, your clothes must be black. Not blue, not charcoal, not pinstripe–formal black. Uber and Lyft drivers may not want to wear a full formal chauffeur uniform, but the basic principles of cleanliness and neatness still apply. Nobody wants to sit in a car with a smelly, sloppy driver, and unwashed sweats are hardly appropriate for work.

The Suit

The most expensive suits are not the best suits for this profession (all the better, since we can't afford them anyway). Go to a department store or national chain store and buy two black suits off the rack with two extra pairs of black pants. Tell the salesperson you need to be able to leave these suits crumpled up in a ball in the corner of your room for days then have them look freshly pressed when you put them on. They will pick the best fabric.

If you have the money, a 100% wool suit is worth the investment. Worsted wool, which is light enough to wear in summer but durable enough for everyday use, is a good choice. Wool is priced according to the number of twists the wool receives during manufacturing (more twists makes for more durability); worsted comes in fabrics ranging from 60-80 twist to super120-twist wool. Polyester and wool blends, as well as microfiber suits, provide a cheaper alternative to wool. Linen and Teflon are not recommended, since they wrinkle and stain quickly.

While many women's suits include skirts instead of pants, such suits are impractical for chauffeuring. A professional chauffeur's suit should be comfortable, and skirts are not conducive to carrying luggage and clambering out of vehicles. Women should invest in a breathable, durable pantsuit rather than a suit with a pencil skirt.

National Stores with Black Suits:

- Overstock.com
- Jos. A Banks
- Burlington Coat Factory
- Men's Wearhouse

Shirt and Shoes

Professional chauffeurs wear only crisp and clean white (never ivory) collared long-sleeved dress shirts under their suit jackets. They wear dress shoes and shine them regularly. Dark socks look best with black suits and shoes; buy a good selection so you always have a clean pair.

While office-dwelling women often wear heels, female professional chauffeurs need to wear shoes that allow them to move, lift, and walk freely. Comfortable flats that will not easily slip off, such as oxford shoes, are ideal.

Inclement Weather Gear

Rain, snow, sleet, or hail do not excuse unregenerate appearance. The professional chauffeur, or app driver, must anticipate inclement weather and possess the accessories to meet every challenge.

A black uniform raincoat with a cold-weather liner is good for northern climates. I suggest a military raincoat sold at Army/Navy Stores. The sharpest-dressed chauffeurs I know wear black Navy trench coats in the rain. Carry at least two umbrellas as well: a classic black umbrella and a pocket black umbrella.

In climates with very cold and snowy weather, headwear is essential, but it should be as professional and formal as your black suit. A knit stocking cap is not appropriate for any driver, professional chauffeurs or Lyft and Uber drivers alike. A ski hat makes a driver like a mugger in the waiting—this is not a good impression.

An ushanka, also known as a trapper hat, chapka, and sometimes an "Elmer Fudd" (after the iconic Loony Tunes character)–has two flexible flaps, one on each side, with a string or leather tie to connect them either beneath the chin or on top of the hat. A wool newsboy/flatcap hat that fits on top of your head, similar to a beret, is also appropriate. A black scarf, black leather gloves, and earmuffs will keep you warm and impeccably dressed.

Checklist for Professional Chauffeurs

- Two black wool pantsuits
- An extra pair of black pants
- Several white button-down shirts
- Black dress shoes or oxfords
- Many pairs of black socks
- Black Army/Navy raincoat
- Classic or pocket black umbrella
- Ushanka or newsboy cap
- Black scarf
- Black leather gloves
- Earmuffs

2) Appearance of *Your* Vehicle

Whether you drive the same company car each day, get a different vehicle each morning, or use your own vehicle, *you are responsible for the way the vehicle looks.* Unlike cab or shuttle vans, chauffeured luxury vehicles have to be spotless. While climate conditions can make it challenging to keep the exterior of the vehicle clean, there is absolutely no excuse for a dirty vehicle interior. If your company charges you with taking the vehicle to the car wash, or if you use your own vehicle, get it washed often. Try to make a friend at the closest car wash so you can get in and out quickly and possibly get extras at a discount.

Professional chauffeurs inspect their vehicle before checking it out from fleet operations at the beginning of their shift. If the company employs auto detailers and cleaners, tip these individuals often to make sure your vehicle is especially clean. If you use your own vehicle, clean it thoroughly before starting each shift.

Car Care Kit

Any driver should carry supplies to keep their vehicle clean in between passengers. In between trips, inspect the rear compartment and clean the carpets, leather, windows, and chrome. Always be sure to clean fingerprints off the glass and door handles; passengers sitting looking out the window during a trip will notice smudges and smears. A disposable lint brush with the roll of sticky tape is a great tool to brush soil and sand off the rear carpet and mats. The best chauffeurs know where the closest commercial vacuums are and use them in between trips throughout their workday.

Perhaps you do not agree that keeping the vehicle clean is your responsibility. Let's put it this way: you are the one who is going to lose any cash tip if your passenger is turned off by a dirty vehicle. If taking five minutes between trips to police the rear compartment is too much, don't be surprised if your customer reviews aren't exceptional or if passengers don't make a habit of requesting you for future trips.

Professional Chauffeur Car Care kit:

- Windex wipes
- Leather wipes
- Paper towels
- Portable vacuum

- Dustpan/brush and or lint tape roll.
- Air freshener spray–new car smell or neutral (no vanilla, no cherry)
- Extra mints, spring water, and napkins

Mechanical or Cosmetic Issues

First, a story to illustrate. One year I went to the biggest livery industry convention sponsored by an industry publication in Atlantic City. I flew in to Philadelphia and booked a luxury sedan to take me from the airport to the hotel in AC. When I got in the sedan, I noticed that the mats were dirty and out of place, and there were no amenities (like spring water, napkins, or mints). Worst of all, when we started driving I heard a terrible air rushing noise coming from the door closest to me. I looked up to see that the rubber seal that is supposed to be between the door and door frame hanging inside the car. So I became curious:

I asked the chauffeur how many trips he had before me.

"None—you are my first," he said.

"Did you pick-up the car at the garage this morning?" I asked.

"Yep," he replied.

When we got to the hotel, he came around and opened the door of the car for me, the rubber seal flapping down as he did. Even though it was in his line of sight, I pointed it out to him.

"Oh, I didn't notice that," he said.

Four days later the convention was over, and I stood outside on the curb at the hotel waiting for a sedan to take me back to the Philadelphia

Airport. My ride pulled up, and to my surprise it was the same driver with the same car. The mats were still dirty, and the same rubber trim was hanging down from the rear passenger door. The sad part about this experience is that the livery company that owned this vehicle was the show sponsor and probably paid $15,000 to $20,000 for that title to promote their company to everyone coming to the livery industry's premier convention.

So, the company owners paid money to promote themselves, but seemingly ignored the fundamental and basic elements of the service delivery experience. Kind of like a restaurant paying for a full-page ad in the New Yorker and serving subpar food. Why bother? I will not use that company again.

First and foremost, we are in the business of safely and comfortably delivering passengers from point A to point B in a refined environment. The best professional chauffeurs I know do not compromise when it comes to the mechanical, cleanliness, or cosmetic condition of the vehicles they pilot.

Some of you may think that their passengers won't notice issues. I can assure you they will. If you are responsible for fixing mechanical or cosmetic issues, handle them as fast as possible when they arise, no matter how trivial they seem. If your company has a mechanic or service manager, diligently inform them of problems so that the vehicle can be fixed. If you use your own vehicle, take it into the mechanic or body shop and fix problems. You will have to pay, but your car will look nicer and work better; this may translate into better tips.

> **Mechanical / cosmetic Issues passengers complain about:**
>
> – Missing, dirty, or disturbed mats
>
> – Check Engine Light on the instrument panel
>
> – Rips or tears in leather, carpet, mats, or headliner
>
> – Accessories not functioning properly
>
> – Noises, exhaust, strange odors in the vehicle

If you work for a company that allows mechanical or cosmetic issues to go unaddressed or has a laissez-faire attitude toward fleet maintenance, you may want to apply to work at a different company. The best companies in the livery business treat their vehicles like thoroughbred racehorses and meticulously maintain them. These companies realize the key to long-term customers is mastering passenger satisfaction and maintaining equipment.

Accuracy

A good chauffeur has a lot in common with an airline pilot. Some people chuckle when I say that, but the parallels are there. We both must thoroughly inspect our vehicle prior to starting the first trip. We must constantly refresh, refuel, and re-inspect between trips. When we are at the controls, we must pay close attention to the instrument panel, speed, and performance of the vehicle as well as traffic around us. Finally, we are both responsible for the lives and comfort of passengers. Luckily for the professional chauffeur, our "pre-flight" checklist is shorter, and our takeoffs and landings are easier. However, success as a chauffeur and as a pilot depends on accuracy and attention to detail.

Accuracy starts with correct and complete trip information, such as passenger names, pick-up and drop-off locations. Many service problems can be traced to the chauffeur's not having complete or accurate information or a chauffeur's failure to read special instructions before accepting the trip. I recommend that chauffeurs verify the details of every trip with dispatchers, or directly with the passenger via a pre-trip confirmation call. Follow your company's Standard Operating Procedures, and be sure they approve your calling the passenger directly prior to the trip. Verifying all information is crucial to your success.

Many companies email or text reservation information to chauffeurs. The best chauffeurs I know take notes and write out trip information, then call to verify the details. This may sound tedious or unnecessary, but it pays off. If something goes wrong, the chauffeur gets the blame and pays the price in lost tips.

- **If receiving trip assignments verbally by smartphone or radio, repeat everything back to and take notes of all details.**

- **If receiving trip assignments on paper, verify all the details of each trip assignment with dispatchers or, if possible, with passengers directly.**

- **If receiving trip assignments via smartphone text or email, print or write out all the details and contact dispatchers or the customer and verify everything.**

Pay specific attention to street addresses and phone numbers and repeat back all addresses. Always repeat back every phone number associated with each trip assignment. Note the actual pick-up time and drop-off time on trip sheets or in the reservations system, as well as in your notes.

1) Knowing Your Area

When I was responsible for the daily operation of my transportation companies, I never hired a chauffeur who just moved to the area—with one exception. I was impressed by a candidate who told me that he had just moved to the area two months before, but that he had spent the last month familiarizing himself with the area. He challenged me to give him an address and see if he could find it. I did, he found it—and he got the job. He went on to be one of my best chauffeurs and, eventually, my training coordinator.

Your company, your dispatcher, and your passengers expect you to know where you are going, the best route to get there, and how long it's going to take on every trip in all kinds of weather and traffic. Use your smartphone, the vehicle navigation, a GPS, or Mapquest to help you. However, if you depend on them all the time in front of your customer, it reflects negatively on you and will negatively affect your income, because you look like an amateur at what you do. Imagine going to a golfing instructor at a local country club and finding him with a club in one hand and a copy of Ben Hogan's book "Five Lessons" in the other. Will you think he knows what he is doing? That is what your passenger thinks as you squint to look at your smartphone or GPS while driving.

If you must use a GPS, don't have it plugged in to your car lighter and stuck to the windshield below the rearview mirror! Nothing says amateur like a driver who displays a GPS in view of passengers. Put the GPS on the left side of the steering wheel, on the far corner of the windshield, down very low.

In your vehicle, to your passengers, you are SIRI—and you'd better be right more than she is. Use technological aids before the passenger gets in the car. If you are dispatched for a last-minute job, map out your route before you pick-up the passenger. Make a cheat sheet on your palm if you have to, and discreetly glance at it (I got through

The Qualities of a Professional Chauffeur

sophomore philosophy in Catholic high school that way).

It is perfectly OK to verify the route with your passenger when they are comfortably seated in the car as you are preparing to get underway, but do so in a definitive manner. "I have us going up Route 93 to Trupelo Road, then turning left. Is that OK, or would you prefer another route?" Even if you didn't know how to get to the address yesterday, appear to know before the passenger gets in your car today.

If you don't know your way around, or you are new to a particular area:

a) Get the largest paper map of your area and study it. A paper map with a scale helps you visualize routes and estimate times.

b) Learn all the highways and major urban and suburban thoroughfares in your area. At a minimum, you must know all major highways and exits in your area. You should also know the major multi-lane streets in every city or town in your territory.

c) Learn where all the concert and sports venues are, as well as hotels and malls. You must also know the protocols for drop-off and pick-up at these locations and know how long it takes to get in and out of these areas during events and at peak traffic times.

d) Study all the airports in your area. Since driving passengers to and from the airport represents roughly 33% of the chauffeured transportation industry, the professional chauffeur must know the ins and outs of every airport in their territory. That includes drop-off and pick-up locations for each airline and baggage claim area. You must know where limousines are allowed to park and wait. You cannot know too much about the airport.

2) Punctuality

Being a professional chauffeur has everything to do with proper timing and punctuality. Unlike the average job where you just have to get there on time in the morning, being a professional chauffeur requires one to be on time to each ride throughout the day. You must pick-up your company car on time, interface with dispatchers in between trips on time, call passengers to confirm (if company policy) on time, be at the pick-up location on time, complete each trip in the allotted time, call in to the office or status on your smartphone to get your next job on time, fill in your paperwork or daily reports on time, etc.

If you are perpetually late, this may not be the career for you. Conversely, if you are always aware of the time, always on time or early to appointments, and always respect the time of others, you may have what it takes.

3) Be Organized

When I get into a livery vehicle, the first thing I do is look at the front passenger seat. If I see paperwork and debris all over the seat, I know I am dealing with a disorganized chauffeur. Imagine going to a five-star restaurant and seeing a server come over with paper hanging out of her pockets, scrambling to find an order pad and pencil. That is what the novice chauffeur looks like when the front seat has stuff all over it.

The professional chauffeur still uses a briefcase or neat computer bag and he keeps everything in it and closed to the eyes of judgmental passengers. Again, the guest wants a clean, refined environment and your possessions should not be part of it. If they are, they need to be very neat and moveable and a moment's notice. What if the passenger prefers to sit up front? The last thing he wants to see is a delay while

The Qualities of a Professional Chauffeur

the chauffeur tries to clean up after himself. The most activity he wants to see is you close your briefcase and quickly put it in the trunk.

"Proper Planning and Preparation Prevents Piss-Poor Performance." This old adage originated in the British Army. Educators and trainers in military or civilian situations find this phrase, nicknamed "The Seven P's," useful. The entire industry of chauffeured transportation depends on Proper Planning and Preparation to Assure Quality Service. ("Three P's, a Q and an S" just doesn't have the same ring as "The Seven P's," though.) Chauffeurs must take a diligent and active role in planning their days and all the details of each trip.

Prior planning starts with planning your workweek, which starts 48 to 72 hours prior to the start of the pay week. You need to let your company know what hours you are available and manage your private matters around that schedule. Chauffeurs who routinely change their schedule midweek impede the overall operation of the company. A professional chauffeur plans her or his week, and unless an emergency pops up, does not deviate from it.

Planning your day starts with making sure your appearance and accessories are in order. If you must pick your vehicle up, thoroughly prepare it at the office, accept your first trips for the day, and map them out. A take-home car is a privilege some companies bestow on their best chauffeurs. If you are fortunate enough to have a company car at home, or if you use your own vehicle, ready it before you leave your driveway.

Proper planning extends to every detail of the interior of the vehicle. Each time a new passenger gets in to the vehicle, he or she must experience a perfectly clean environment with no traces of the prior passenger. The second the last passenger exits, you must plan for the next passenger.

4) Reliable

Professional chauffeurs get driving assignments with several hours' or even a day's advance notice. More often than not, though, you will be dispatched with little notice at all. In either case, you are expected to perform in an exemplary fashion and provide your passenger with quality service. So, you must be reliable and solve your own problems as they occur without constantly calling dispatchers (or worse, passengers) for assistance.

You must be prepared for anything. Plan on going to unfamiliar areas: have maps, a GPS, a smartphone app. Plan on messes: have cleaning supplies in the trunk of your car. Plan on being dispatched with incomplete trip details. Have other chauffeurs' cell numbers at the ready *to ask them for assistance instead of calling the office*. Planes will be late and flight numbers will be wrong, so have the public information phone number to all the airports you service and the local phone numbers of every airline check-in desk at each airport. The more reliable and prepared you are, the more successful you will be.

ALERTNESS

When you have guests in your vehicle, you must be acutely aware of your surroundings outside the vehicle and the comfort of your passengers inside the vehicle. You must be alert at all times, especially when driving in neighborhoods or moving at high speeds.

By keeping the environment inside the vehicle calm while scanning the road constantly, you can avoid accidents and ensure a comfortable trip for your passenger. Avoid having the stereo playing too loud so you can hear what is going on *inside and* outside the vehicle (sirens from emergency vehicles, screeching tires from other vehicles, or cross walk signals from pedestrian traffic). Quiet and calming also includes not initiating long, distracting conversations with passengers so you can focus on the road and be totally aware of your surroundings. You don't have to be rude to limit distractions; if passengers ask you questions or wish to converse, simply limit your answers to a sentence or two and a smile. When passengers are speaking about the trip, their destination, or future trips, it is critical that you listen and repeat what they told you and let them know that when you stop you will ask them to confirm what they said so you can write down notes.

1) Ability to "Pilot" Safely

When I road test chauffeurs, I tell them to pretend that we have twelve eggs in a dish on the rear seat. Their job is to a) follow all the traffic rules and b) not break the eggs. Driving well is the first skill required to be a professional chauffeur. A professional chauffeur never speeds, never tailgates, never cuts off other drivers, and never slams on the brakes. He or she always uses blinkers and always obeys traffic signs and parking rules. If you have bad driving habits, change them, or it will negatively affect your income.

If you have numerous at-fault accidents, speeding tickets, or a history of other moving violations on your driving record, you may want to consider another career. Is a bad driving record the end of the road for you as a chauffeur? Maybe, maybe not. If your community requires chauffeurs to have a special license through your state, city, or other local agency, your driving record must meet their requirements. If there are no such special license requirements, you still must present your driving record to any prospective employer so they can clear it through their commercial insurance carrier. Many livery companies have internal rules that stipulate no accidents, speeding tickets, or other moving violations for five to seven years.

Request a copy of your complete driving record from the Department of Motor Vehicles and have it in hand when you apply for a chauffeur license. Give a copy to any prospective employer as well.

2) Ability to "Pilot" Safely with Passengers in the Vehicle

A professional chauffeur knows the difference between piloting and driving and demonstrates this behind the wheel. If your driving record is clean of citations but you just haven't been caught routinely speeding and driving recklessly, you won't last as a professional chauffeur unless you modify your driving behavior.

I'm using the term piloting because piloting a vehicle with passengers requires more skills and awareness than driving a vehicle alone. When you drive your car without passengers, you are responsible for your own safety and the safety of other drivers and passengers on the road. When you pilot a vehicle with paying passengers, you are not only responsible for the safety of yourself, your company vehicle, and others on the road; you are responsible for the safety, comfort, and enjoyment of the passengers inside your car. Getting guests from point A to point B without an accident does not mean you are good at piloting a vehicle. Your guest is judging your driving performance with every movement of the steering wheel.

When chauffeuring passengers, you must always be aware of your surroundings, your vehicle speed and position, the vehicles around you, and the comfort and safety of your guests. Piloting means being totally aware of the vehicle and passengers in your care. It is the constant movement of your eyes between your three mirrors, front and rear windshields, and console gauges. It is listening for sounds inside and outside your vehicle and anticipating the feel of the road. It is not engaging in conversations, looking at your cell phone or GPS, or listening to sports radio or your favorite songs. These things distract you from your charge.

The #1 Customer Complaint with Chauffeured Transportation: Poor Driving

The Qualities of a Professional Chauffeur

ATTITUDE

If I said having a smile on your face, looking sharp, and displaying a positive attitude could get you 20% to 30% more income, would you say I was crazy? Let me put it this way: have you ever seen bad attitudes rewarded?

Restaurant industry research shows that servers with positive attitudes earn on average 15% MORE in tips than those who deliver the same overall quality of service with neutral attitudes. It stands to reason that a chauffeur who displays a positive attitude to passengers will be rewarded more than a chauffeur with an indifferent attitude.

After working hundreds of hours in the busiest dispatching departments in this industry, I have come to the irrefutable conclusion that dispatchers are more inclined to give a chauffeur with a positive attitude more trips than indifferent chauffeurs. If you expect positive outcomes and results, and you usually get them.

A positive attitude has many benefits. It promotes overall positive mental health and coping skills. When you turn every challenge into an opportunity, life is more fun.

Others perceive positive people differently as well. Positive workers inspire and motivate others. You will be perceived as a leader, and generally those with a positive attitude receive more raises, bonuses, and gratuities. Other employees around you will also adopt a positive work attitude, making it easier for everyone to get along during stressful situations.

How to Build a Positive Attitude

Positivity at work starts at home. If you are not a naturally positive person, start by taking care of yourself: eating well, exercising, and getting enough sleep. Develop a habit of using only positive words, and surround yourself with positive people. Celebrate successes (even the small ones) and look for the good in every person and challenging situation. Smile and laugh throughout the day.

Prepare for success at work by setting goals for yourself. Get plenty of rest before a shift, and get your clothes, cleaning kit, and other supplies ready in advance. Pack healthy snacks, water, and reading material such as a lighthearted book or magazine.

While at work, perform your duties with passion and enthusiasm. Solve problems without complaining and use your breaks to recharge.

Communication Skills

Chauffeurs must be extremely good listeners and have excellent communication skills. Every aspect of doing this job properly involves listening and communication.

Good communication skills require a high level of self-awareness. Understanding your personal style of communicating will help you to create positive impressions with your passengers and good working relationships with company staff.

As a professional chauffeur, you must not only be adept at listening but also good at taking discreet notes and repeating vital information back to your dispatcher and passengers. Even if you have a good memory, taking notes lets you capture even the smallest detail and recite it back to your charge. We will discuss communication and listening more later.

Anticipation

The most important of the five A's for creating successful service experience is anticipation. Part of your job during the ride, along with

The Qualities of a Professional Chauffeur

safe driving, is observing the passenger and finding a way to wow her by providing something she may want or need but did not ask for.

Anticipating is a combination of observing your guests, using common sense, and putting yourself in their shoes. If your passenger is fumbling in a computer bag or pockets, offer him a pen. If he has his cell phone out, mention that you have several car charges for different types of phones in the armrest console. Keep a fresh pad of paper handy in case a guest wants it. Perhaps on a particularly rainy day you pack extra umbrellas, anticipating one of your guests may need one.

In addition to being observant, put yourself in your passenger's position. If you got off a five-hour flight, what would you want? If you were being picked up at your home at 5:00 a.m. to catch a 7:00 a.m. flight, what would you need?

Anticipating the needs of passengers comes with experience. You will get the hang of it over time if you are in tune to what you are doing. The goal is to wow each guest so she will want to use your services again.

Anticipate that passenger might be thirsty for something other than spring water and carry a cooler of sodas, or anticipate they will be hungry and carry small packages of crackers, or anticipate that they might want to freshen up after a long flight and offer them hard candies, mints, or chewing gum. You can leave anticipation to chance or come prepared. I chose the latter when I drove guests.

Extra "Anticipation Kit"

- Pens, pencils, and note paper
- A collection of car chargers for different types of phones. If you want to be really high tech, you can go to an auto parts store and by a 12-volt DC to 110 volt AC converter, which makes

your cigarette lighter a plug-in outlet.

- Small cans or bottles of soda, juice, and coffee (get them at a bulk food store like Costco for the best deal)
- Snacks, such as crackers, nuts, or fruit (also available at bulk food stores)
- Candy and chewing gum (also available at bulk food stores)
- Extra umbrellas

THE SERVICE EXPERIENCE

The professional chauffeur executes what the customer is paying for: a superior experience during every trip. The customer chose an expensive transportation service. If the customer wanted the fastest trip possible, she or he might have called a cab or driven a personal vehicle. If the customer were primarily concerned with cost, he or she might have asked a spouse or colleague for a ride or called a multi-stop shuttle van service. When customers hire a professionally chauffeured vehicle, they expect a superior, more convenient, more efficient, and more pleasurable experience.

Customers will not remember the reservationist who took their initial call, credit the dispatcher with getting the car there on time, or judge the company president for choosing the wrong route. Like it or not, they will credit the chauffeur for how well or badly the trip went. I have been picked up late for a trip and listened as the driver blamed the dispatcher. I have been dropped off at the wrong airline and had the driver blame the reservations staff. I did not think positively about either of these experiences.

Many chauffeurs I meet either forget or don't realize that what they do before, during, and after the trip makes or breaks the customer experience. It builds clientele and impacts the company's reputation.

The Qualities of a Professional Chauffeur

A professional chauffeur does everything possible to make sure every drive goes smoothly. They search for addresses prior and calculate arrival times before each trip. They verify destinations with customers either on a confirmation call to the passenger or as soon as the customer gets in the car. The best chauffeurs leave nothing to chance and set themselves up to succeed on every trip.

View each trip as a chance to create a positive customer experience. The vehicle plays a large role, but the chauffeur makes each trip an experience. Your performance is critical.

Service experiences are personal. They elicit emotions and are memorable. Great service experiences leave a lasting impression. They are compared and judged and repeated to other people. As a professional chauffeur, your ultimate goal is to create as many memorable experiences for passengers as possible, so they will recommend you to others, grow your individual repeat clientele, and bolster the image of your company.

Think about a time when you enjoyed a delicious meal at a great restaurant, prepared by a professional chef and served by a professional waiter. Think about how you were greeted and seated. Recall how the wait staff met your needs, was attentive, and hit every service cue. All this–not just the food–combines to make the entire experience memorable.

Now, think of a negatively memorable experience. You may still feel disappointed or angry about it, even well after it occurred. Human nature is such that we repeat or retell the negative experience to others on average 20 times more than we extol favorable experiences. Your performance of creating positive experiences (and avoiding negative ones) is vital.

We earn our reputation one experience at a time. If you approach your job as that of a driver, you will be treated like a taxi driver. Your customer's experience will be more like a taxi ride—and your extra gratuity compensation will show that.

Things to Master from Chapter Three:

- To be a professional chauffeur, you have to like taking care of people—PERIOD.
- If you think serving others is beneath you, you are in the wrong industry—PERIOD.
- You must have Service DNA to excel in the service industry. Don't have it? GET OUT.
- You cannot fake liking to take care of people OR having Service DNA.
- To be a professional chauffeur and increase your income you must master the Five A's: Appearance, Accuracy, Alertness, Attitude, and <u>above all, Anticipation</u>.
- Focus on creating a superior service experience.

CHAPTER FOUR

The Four Steps of the Drive

FOUR STEPS TO PROVIDING A SUCCESSFUL TRIP

There are four stages to each trip that, if properly executed, make it a successful service experience. These are solely in the hands of the professional chauffeur.

The Four Steps of the Drive:

1) Preparation
2) The Greeting
3) The Ride
4) The Close

1. Preparation

The professional chauffeur should be equipped with more than just keys and a wallet.

The Professional Chauffeur Kit:

- Smartphone

- Maps
    - Local street maps (always out of view of the passengers)
    - Printed directions for each trip
    - GPS unit (always out of sight of the passengers)
    - AAA map of the entire country (always out of view of the passengers)
- Attraction guidebook and a Zagat restaurant guide
- Office Supplies
    - Pens
    - Note paper
    - Credit card charge forms
    - Business cards
    - A calculator
    - Blank receipts
- Amenities
    - Bottle opener
    - Breath mints
    - Lint brush
    - CDs or an MP3 player
    - Magazines
    - Extra umbrellas

- Small first aid kit
- Accident kit
    - Insurance documents
    - Vehicle registration
    - Accident form for your company
    - Local law enforcement agency contact information
- A flashlight
- Cleaning Supplies
    - Paper towels
    - Glass cleaner
    - Whisk broom
    - A lint brush with the sticky roll of tape

Staging *Your* Vehicle

Each passenger expects a spotless vehicle to pick them up. In some cases, the weather may not always cooperate. However, on sunny dry days, there is absolutely no excuse for your vehicle to be dirty.

Assuming you start your shift with a clean vehicle exterior, it is part of your job to make sure it remains as clean as the weather allows. Keep cleaning supplies in the trunk of the vehicle, and also know where every express wash is around the city. In between trips on sunny days, roll through a car wash and dry the exterior. Just like you would top off your gas tank to make sure you won't run out of gas, get a car wash to meet your customers' expectations of a clean vehicle.

On rainy days, at least make sure the exterior of the vehicle is free of fingerprints, smudges, or any dirt that could get on the passengers' clothing as they enter and exit the vehicle. Passengers understand during rainy or snowy weather, the exterior of your vehicle may not be perfectly clean. However, they don't expect to get dirty using your service.

Interior of the Vehicle

Imagine if you walked in to a hotel room and found the bathroom dirty, with used towels on the floor. Would you want to sleep in the room? Neither would I. Then why do some chauffeurs think it is perfectly OK that the second, third, fourth passengers of the day see dirty mats, trash in the ashtray, and fingerprints on the window?

One major complaint from repeat passengers of livery services is dirty vehicles. One time, I got a call from an irate passenger who used our service. When she got home and hung up her raincoat, she noticed dirt and grime on the side and attributed it to our vehicle. I apologized for the incident and told the client I would dispatch a car and driver to her home to pick-up the coat and bring it right to the dry cleaner. I promised to return it the next morning clean as a whistle. We did just that, and she was completely satisfied with that resolution.

When the driver got back to the garage at the end of his shift, I checked the car myself. Indeed, on the bottom of the passenger door in the doorjamb was a big smear of what looked like a mixture of grease and dirt about the size of a shoe. It probably came from a trailer or construction vehicle during the day.

I asked the driver about it, and he claimed he never saw it. The detailer who cleaned the vehicle that morning before it left the yard said the grease was absolutely not there that morning. It was clear the driver never inspected the vehicle in between trips. It was a rookie mistake that cost the company labor and a dry-cleaning bill.

The Four Steps of the Drive

Ultimately, vehicles with a dirty interior hurt the chauffeur most. Regardless of the weather outside, passengers expect the interior of your vehicle to be spotlessly clean, with no signs of the previous passenger. If I am picked up in a vehicle with a dirty interior, I never add to the tip. In some cases, I have asked my office to call the provider and remove the tip entirely. Most people don't do that; I do it because I am in the business, and I am a fanatic about good customer service. Normally customers just choose another company the next time they need a ride.

Before Your Shift: Even if your company has a detailer who preps the vehicles at the beginning of each day, ultimately it is part of your job as a professional chauffeur to make certain the interior environment of the vehicle is always clean. At the beginning of your shift, check the interior of the vehicle and make sure that everything the passenger can see is immaculate. This includes the front seats and rear deck behind the passenger seat.

What do you do when you check out a vehicle and find the detailer has not cleaned it or there are mechanical issues? If you find that the vehicle is improperly staged or there is some kind of mechanical issue, you should in all cases to report the problem with the staging or mechanical issue with the vehicle to management. If the mechanical issue will impair the vehicle in any way, you are to immediately report the problem to management, who should assign you another vehicle.

In Between Trips: As a professional chauffeur, policing the interior of your vehicle is pretty easy. Simply keep a small cleaning kit in the trunk. I recommend a soft-sided cooler with a zipper. To clean vehicles on the fly, you only need four things:

1) Paper towels

2) Glass cleaner

3) Whisk broom

4) A lint brush with the sticky roll of tape

Checklist:

- Remove any trash from the area and check the ashtray, cup holders, and any slide-out drawers for debris
- Shake out the mats using the whisk broom, brush the carpet, and get as much of the debris out with the broom as you can, and then use the lint brush to get the remainder
- Spray the glass, the door, and the door sill with the window cleaner
- Wipe down the seat with a damp paper towel
- Sit in the seat (with your feet outside the vehicle) and take a passenger's view of the vehicle to make sure everything is spotless

Other Tips for in Between Trips:

- Move the front passenger seat forward to give your passenger the most space
- Test all vehicle controls front and back and make sure they work properly
- Set interior climate at 72 degrees and set the stereo low on an easy listening station.
- Reset amenities like magazines, spring water, and mints

Trunks and Doorjambs/Sills:

In many cases, we carry passengers to the airport with luggage or around town with baggage or packages. Professional chauffeurs always

The Four Steps of the Drive

keep the trunk of their vehicles neat at all times in case passengers walk back to the rear of the vehicle. Keep any personal belongings in the corner of the trunk and keep your cleaning kit closed and orderly.

Another area that often gets overlooked is doorjambs and sills. When passengers get in and out of your vehicle, regardless of which door they choose, the doorjamb and doorsill should be just as clean as the interior of the vehicle (remember the customer with the rain coat?).

2. The Greeting

Phone Call

The perfect greeting sets the tone for the trip well before you meet the passenger. Many professional chauffeurs call their passengers either the night before or morning of to confirm trip details and see if the passenger would like anything special in the vehicle for the trip. Some companies may have office staff do this or have different policies, so ask your supervisor if this is appropriate.

Be Punctual

Part of the perfect greeting is also your proper and timely arrival. It is customary on pre-reserved trips for you to arrive 15 minutes prior to the pick-up time. In the industry this is called the "spot time." This is done for a variety of reasons, but most importantly, it reassures anxious passengers that their vehicles will arrive in a timely fashion.

Your company will typically dictate the time of arrival, but it never hurts to be 15 minutes early. When picking up at a residence, some chauffeurs park a block away and pull up to the actual house ten minutes prior to the actual pick-up time so as not to rush the passenger.

Properly driving up and parking the vehicle is also critically important. I usually recommend backing the vehicle in the driveway just enough to get it off the street and putting it in park while keeping the engine running. At this point, make a final check: the vehicle should be clean and at a comfortable temperature, and the stereo should be off or on low on an easy listening station.

Positioning and Greeting

Once you exit the vehicle, you should be positioned standing with the trunk open next to the back door of the vehicle. When picking up at a residence, it is proper to ring the doorbell five minutes prior to the pick-up time if the passenger does not acknowledge your presence.

When you meet the passenger, use his full name and address your passenger in a cheerful, friendly tone. Use:

Mr. and Mrs., sir, madam, or ma'am for adults

Young man, Young lady for children

Something like "Good morning, Mr. Jones," is fine. If you have driven the passenger before, tell him that it is good to see him again. If you don't know the passenger but they have used the service before, thank him for using the service again.

I always ask the passenger if I can carry her luggage to the car, but for safety reasons, it is a good idea to let her carry the luggage to the entry to their house. I do not recommend going inside the house to get luggage.

It is customary to open the rear door(s) for all passengers and wait to close the door(s) until they are comfortably seated.

In the Car

Check/verify the information on each of your trips. This is critically important to the success of the trip and looking professional as you greet each passenger before the trip.

If the passenger rides with you frequently, remember his likes and dislikes. Have his favorite drink ready. Have his favorite newspaper waiting in the center of the rear seat.

Always break the ice when you get in the driver seat. Ask your client how she is doing. Confirm her destination and special instructions before you start moving. You will either look professional because you have thoroughly checked the trip instructions or look bad because the passenger has to correct you.

Things to say before putting the vehicle in drive:

a) *Do you have a preference as to our route today?*

b) *May I acquaint you with some of the features and amenities?*

c) *Is the temperature OK?*

d) *Is there a radio station you would like to listen to?*

3. THE RIDE

Be Quiet (for Goodness' Sake, Be Quiet)

The second biggest complaint about new chauffeurs is they feel the need to talk the entire trip. When your initial greeting is complete, stop talking and focus on driving. If the passenger wants to talk, let her continue the conversation! Don't assume she wants to chat the whole trip. In general, speak only when spoken to. Your passengers may want to get some rest or need to collect their thoughts.

I cannot tell you the number of trips I have personally taken where the chauffeur talked too much, but it has been quite a few. I am not sure whether I look like a lonely guy, but some of these drivers talked nonstop about subjects I had no interest in and never brought up.

I can, however, tell you the exact number of complaints I received about chatty drivers between 2010 and 2014: 41, involving 14 drivers. Nine of those drivers were counseled and we never got another complaint about them again on any performance issues. The other five were eventually terminated for receiving complaints from other passengers about the same kind of thing repeatedly.

In one case, the offending chauffeur chatted up everyone in the company in person and by phone. You just could not get away from him. Looking back, I think we should have known he had a problem long before we received a customer complaint.

The circumstances were this: we routinely surveyed many passengers about our performance immediately after they took trips. One time we surveyed a customer by phone the day after the trip. She commented that the chauffeur said that he had a degree in finance from XYZ University and was between jobs and only drove for us because he needed the money. Apparently, he also told her he was the best chauffeur we had and he could run the company better than our managers but we could not pay him enough compared to his prior jobs. We terminated him the same day.

Know when to listen and when to stay mute. When in doubt, be quiet. I can tell you I never heard anyone complain about a chauffeur being too ***quiet!***

The Four Steps of the Drive

Matching and Mirroring (Master This, Please)

A surefire way to avoid ever getting a complaint about being chatty is to use a technique I learned from a career in sales called "matching and mirroring." Let the passenger or guest set the tone for the ride. If he talks or asks you a question, you respond and continue the dialogue with another comment. Match the passenger's conversational style and mirror his responses with your own. If after the icebreaker "How are you doing today?" the passenger opens dialogue on an appropriate subject, simply respond to them and wait and see if they respond back. If on the other hand, after you say "How is your day going?" she responds with one word, it is likely that she don't want to speak. You should mirror this also.

Never Bring Up Personal Stuff (Never, Never, Never)

The subject matter of conversations should never be personal. Beyond asking how someone's day is going, the professional chauffeur displays reticence and never asks any personal questions. If the passenger asks you personal questions, keep the conversation professional.

Safe Driving

Universally in the chauffeured transportation business, the number one complaint from passengers is poor driving. It is my contention that we are a society of bad drivers—or at least a society of careless drivers who follow strict traffic rules when we know the police are right behind us. Put my theory to the test someday when you have a trip that lasts longer than an hour. Watch how other people drive and I bet you will notice five acts of poor driving before the trip ends.

To avoid passenger complaints about poor driving, focus on being a safe driver all the time. Not just when you have passengers, but every time when you are behind the wheel of any vehicle. We have devoted an entire chapter to safe driving, so we will leave it at that for now.

The Perfect Close

For the first fifteen years of my career in corporate America, I managed sales people. I taught them how to "close the sale" so the company gained revenue and they earned their commission. I could teach someone the fundamentals of selling, but if they did not know how to close the sale, they didn't make money. Our goal as individual sales people was to develop the "perfect close." In the transportation industry, the "perfect close" is different than a sales close, but performing it properly is important if you want big tips.

The close is the final step in the ride and end of the passenger's service experience. If the other three steps were performed properly, this step has the most impact on whether passengers will book their next trip with your company, request you as their driver, or refer our company to friends.

The perfect close requires you to safely deliver your passenger to their destination, put the vehicle in park, disembarked the passenger, and unloaded any luggage and belongings. The professional chauffeur knows that the job is not over just because the vehicle is in park. Our guest is paying for service, not a bum rush out of the vehicle. Taxi drivers may pull up to the curb, turn their head and signal the passenger to get out, but professional chauffeurs know there is more expected of them.

Disembarking

Once the vehicle is in park at the passenger's destination, the chauffeur asks the passengers to stand by inside the vehicle. The chauffeur exits the vehicle, walks around back of the vehicle, and opens the trunk if there is luggage to be removed. The chauffeur then opens the passenger's door. If the passenger is elderly, the chauffeur extends a forearm and offers to help the passenger exit the vehicle.

Once the passenger is out of the vehicle, the chauffeur walks her to the trunk so she can watch the luggage being removed and make sure everything is accounted for. When the luggage is out of the trunk, the professional chauffeur takes it all to the front door of the establishment, be it a home, hotel, or airport. Never shut the trunk until the passenger has reached the door.

Disembarking Suggestions:

- When pulling in to a driveway at night to disembark a passenger, pull straight ahead so that your headlights light the way to the house. Always carry an umbrella in the rain and a flashlight to assist the passenger to their door.

- When pulling up to an airport terminal with multiple guests, always disembark passengers sitting on the driver's side in the rear seat first and shield them from vehicles going by. Guide them to the curb and disembark the rest of the passengers.

- Before leaving, check the passenger compartment and trunk for any personal belongings they have left behind.

The Goodbye

Each passenger has many options for transportation, but they chose your company and you were chosen to represent your company. Thus, the passenger deserves a sincere thank you using their full name. Here is your foolproof closing line:

"Thank you for riding with [company] today, Ms. Smith. It has been my pleasure to serve your transportation needs. Is there anything else I can assist you with before I depart?"

Whether your company surveys customers or not, you can "self survey" to get some feedback. Your last question as you assist your passengers out of the vehicle at the curb on an airport trip should be:

"Was everything satisfactory about my performance today?"

If they say "yes," you should respond,

"It has been my pleasure taking care of your transportation today. Please use us again and request me as your chauffeur if you'd like."

I have found that chauffeurs who consistently use the "self-survey" technique are tipped more than the average chauffeur. The technique shows passengers that you care about your performance and thus care about the passenger. It is also a natural segue for the passenger to reach in to their pocket and perhaps tip extra if they indeed answered "yes."

Ideally, you want the service experience to be so good that passengers answer the above question with an overwhelming, "Yes! Absolutely, your service was wonderful. Thank You."

What do you do if they say "no"? First of all, apologize for whatever the issue was regardless of how trivial or serious. Thank them for the feedback and let them know you will try to change. For example, if someone says, "Honestly, I was getting a bit seasick because you kept slamming on the brakes," start by apologizing. Say that you did not realize you were doing that and pledge to work on it. Assure them it will not happen again if you drive them in the future. You would be surprised how many repeat passengers request a chauffeur they initially had a complaint about if the chauffeur uses this technique.

Before leaving the area, check the rear passenger compartment of the vehicle and the trunk. If this passenger is a local resident, they have the potential to be a repeat passenger; record their likes and dislikes on your trip sheets or in a notebook for future reference.

Multi-Stop Trips

In many cases, you will spend a whole evening, a whole day, or perhaps several days as a personal driver for the same guest. This may happen if an important businessperson or celebrity is in town, or it could simply be a group of friends enjoying a night out to a restaurant and a game. Whatever the case, these trips require some additional steps.

Contact Person: If there are multiple guests (such as a in a group night out or a corporate entertainment party), establish a principal person to communicate with. For corporate groups, this will probably be the event coordinator or an administrative assistant. For private groups, it will probably be the person who made the reservation.

The Day Before: Prior to every group assignment, call the passenger (or their executive assistant) to get details. Ask them:

- If you can get anything special (beverages, magazines, etc.)
- If you will be picking people up from different locations (for example, part of the group may be at an airport, part at a hotel)

Amenities: As soon as your passengers are in the vehicle, familiarize them with the amenities and show them how everything works.

Establish a Pick-Up Location and Time: Coordinate the exact pick-up location and times with the passengers. Make sure every guest has this information and get everyone's cell phone number (make sure they have yours, too).

Protect Possessions: Always offer to lock personal possessions of the guests in the trunk before they disembark at the venue.

Restage: After you have dropped off your guests, clean and re-stage your vehicle. Never assume you have time to clean the vehicle later. As soon as you drop off passengers at the beginning of the night, prepare your vehicle for the return trip.

The Silent Judge: Seeking Feedback

Professionals in all fields seek out criticism and critique their own performances to improve. Major league baseball players work with coaches from the first tryout until their final game. Football players watch videos of their past performance on the field to learn how to handle future plays. Pilots spend time on flight simulators every year to renew their licenses. Considering that over 30% of most professional chauffeur income comes from variable compensation and gratuities based on performance, chauffeurs should be just as concerned about performance as other professionals.

"I just drive a car," you may be saying to yourself. "Is this really important?" YES. Remember, servers "just" serve food, but the very best ones earn 15% to 20% more than their peers based solely on their performance. When you self-survey and get feedback from customers, take it seriously. Make changes to your driving and communication styles. You'll get better, and your feedback will become positive the overwhelming majority of the time.

For Operators

I strongly encourage every operator I consult with to survey passengers on every single trip either by email or by a business reply card using the specifics of each and every trip:

The Four Steps of the Drive

Thank you for riding with Maurice to the Los Angeles International Airport on Tuesday, April 1 at 9 a.m. We would like to know how we did and would greatly appreciate your feedback.

1) Was the vehicle on time? Yes No

2) Was the vehicle satisfactory? Yes No

3) Was the chauffeur's driving satisfactory? Yes No

4) Was the chauffeur's performance up to your expectations? Yes No

If you answered "no" on any of the questions, kindly explain why:

___

Surveys don't have to be elaborate to be effective.

Your company may already be asking for feedback on your performance; the smart ones survey passengers all the time and don't necessarily inform chauffeur staff. As Transportation Network Companies (TNCs) become more prevalent in our industry, chauffeur performance feedback and ranking will become critically important for all companies. They make rating drivers commonplace, so naturally if a passenger uses both types of service, they are watching your performance as well as the TNC drivers they encounter.

ABOUT TIPPING OR GRATUITY

According to the Oxford English Dictionary, the word "tip" originated as slang somewhere around the 1500s. It meant to "give a small present of money" for service rendered. The word "gratuity" comes from Latin (*gratuitus*, "free, freely given.") It came to mean "money given for favor or services" in the 1530s. "Give a gratuity to" was first

65

in print in 1706 and the noun "gratuity" emerged in 1755.

The practice of tipping began in England. By the late 16th century, it was expected that overnight guests staying in private homes of the wealthy would give sums of money, known as *vails,* to the host's servants. Soon after, customers began tipping in London coffeehouses, taverns, and other commercial establishments.

In the United States, tips or a gratuity is most prevalent in the hospitality industry, particularly in restaurants and some positions in the lodging sector. In the restaurant industry, bartenders and wait staff are paid a lower hourly wage (sometimes below minimum wage) and a large percentage of their income is derived from tips or gratuities. In these occupations it is commonplace to add between 15% and 20% to your meal for the wait staff gratuity.

As the service sector has evolved over the past several decades, however, an unhealthy entitlement mentality has taken hold. Servers expect gratuity regardless of whether they provide poor or exceptional service. This created very lackluster service performance across the board in moderately priced eating and lodging establishments. Service personnel have no pride in their positions, leading to low patron expectations. I don't think this bodes well for the service industry. Having said that, I believe that the higher cost of the service experience dictates more emphasis on providing good service.

Tipping in the Chauffeured Transportation Industry

Over the past decade in the chauffeured transportation industry, we have tried a variety of pricing and operational models to deal with gratuities. Some companies call it a service charge, others call it a gratuity. Some charge an automatic percentage on top of the charge for the trip, some charge a flat rate. Other operators leave gratuity off the bill entirely, urging passengers to tip in cash at their discretion.

Regardless of your company's stance on gratuities, you can drastically increase your income by focusing, not on the tip, but on providing an exemplary and memorable service experience. I urge everyone who reads this book not to focus on tips. Instead, stand out as the top 10% of the top 10% of professional chauffeurs.

Rules of Gratuity:

a) Amateurs talk about tips

b) Professionals earn their gratuity

c) If you have to talk about gratuity, you have not earned it.

As a chauffeur, you are earning gratuity from the time you get your trip assignment until the time you say goodbye to the passenger. At any point during that transaction, anything can happen that make experience good or bad. Focus on providing excellent service, and the tips will come. If you have to prompt a guest for the gratuity, you have cheapened the experience and have not earned a tip.

In sales we used to say that if you did your job correctly—if you identified the client's needs, properly explained your product or service, built rapport with the client, etc.—then closing the sale was the smallest and most rewarding step. The same is true in chauffeured transportation. If you have done your job correctly and exceeded the passenger's expectations, people will tip you and tip you well.

An Example to Aspire To

The best chauffeur I know, Robin, came to me as a result of an acquisition in 2010. He had a storied 15-year career until he decided that, at 80 years old, he was getting too old to be responsible for driving guests. When I met Robin, he had worked in the business for 30 years. He was an interesting guy and he took his job very seriously. He makes a great example of the actual transaction the professional chauffeur is responsible for providing in our business: the trip.

Robin came in early every day, with his shoes shined and his black briefcase full of everything he needed to prep his vehicle for the day. Even though we employed a staff of detailers at our company, Robin inspected every vehicle before he left the garage. He called it his "white glove test." He checked every interior surface and vacuumed the mats and carpet again and sprayed his own "new car smell" air freshener before he was underway. He checked every trip assignment before he left the office and clarified special instructions and small details with the dispatch and reservations staff.

When I first met Robin, he showed me a small binder he keeps with him in his work vehicle. It had up-to-date clippings of all the sporting events, concerts, and other attractions. "I never want anyone to ask me a question about this area that I don't have the answer to," he explained.

Event information wasn't all that Robin collected. He had a ritual of writing down the names and preferences of every passenger for the trips he was assigned so he could refer to them on subsequent trips and provide little amenities for each customer. He kept blank note cards in his brief case and wrote down specifics on each passenger, such as favorite beverages, snacks, and magazines. If they celebrated a birthday or anniversary on their trip, he was sure to send them a card the following year a month in advance with his business card so they would call and book a limousine (and him) for the upcoming celebration. He made a note card that recorded details of every single trip during his 15-year career as a professional chauffeur. Upon his retirement from our company, he showed me his boxes detailing over 15,000 trips.

Guess what all of this got him? Aside from great personal pride and integrity in his work, Robin was the most requested chauffeur we employed. He also earned more than any other chauffeur I ever met. He truly has Service DNA and was rewarded with happiness, generosity, and gratitude.

Things to Master from Chapter Four:

- Master the Four Steps of the Drive: Preparation, The Greeting, The Ride, and The Close

- Master the concept of matching and mirroring

- How to handle multi-stop trips

- Seek feedback from all customers

- If you ask about a tip, you don't deserve a tip—earn your gratuity instead

CHAPTER FIVE

Knowledge and Communication

I ordered a car in New York recently, and when I got to the airport, my driver was late. His first words:

"Aw man, I am so sorry," he said when he finally arrived. "The f•••••g president is in town again, and he's screwing up all the traffic as usual."

Chauffeuring, like any service industry job, requires good communication skills. When I got into this business, I found that mastering customer service involved a completely different skill set. In my old job, I used to fire people; it was one-way communication. The communication skill set is as important as safe driving.

Communication skills don't just encompass what to say; they also include what you *should not* say. Most mistakes I've seen in the business have to do with not listening to instruction, not listening to the client, and improper communication. There are some jobs that require a lot of verbal communication, but for chauffeurs, most of the emphasis is on holding your tongue. Here are some of the things you should know about communication as a professional chauffeur.

Active Listening

Active listening helps you learn what your passenger needs. There are five key elements of active listening[20]. They all help ensure that you hear the other person, and that the other person knows you are hearing what they say.

1. Pay Attention: Give the speaker your undivided attention and acknowledge the message. Recognize that non-verbal communication also "speaks" loudly.

   - Look at the speaker directly.
   - Put aside distracting thoughts.
   - Don't mentally prepare a rebuttal!
   - Avoid being distracted by environmental factors. For example, side conversations.
   - "Listen" to the speaker's body language.

2. Show That You Are Listening: Use your body language and gestures to convey your attention.

   - Nod occasionally.
   - Smile and use other facial expressions.
   - Note your posture, and make sure it is open and inviting.
   - Encourage the speaker to continue with small verbal comments like yes, and uh-huh.

3. Provide Feedback: Our personal filters, assumptions, judgments, and beliefs can distort what we hear. As a listener, your role is to

---

[20] Ijres.org

understand what is being said. This may require you to reflect what is being said and ask questions.

- Reflect what has been said by paraphrasing. "What I'm hearing is" and "Sounds like you are saying" are great ways to reflect back.

- Ask questions to clarify certain points. "What do you mean when you say." "Is this what you mean?"

- Summarize the speaker's comments periodically.

4. Defer Judgment: Interrupting is a waste of time. It frustrates the speaker and limits full understanding of the message.

- Allow the speaker to finish each point before asking questions.

- Don't interrupt with comments.

5. Respond Appropriately: Active listening is a model for respect and understanding. You are gaining information and perspective.

- Be candid, open, and honest in your response.

- Assert your opinions respectfully.

- Treat the other person in a way that you think he or she would want to be treated.

ACTIVELY OBSERVING

Active observing means paying close attention, not just to what your passenger says, but also to what she does not say. It means noticing broken luggage handles, rumbling stomachs, or empty cigarette packs. This ties back in with anticipation—anticipating passenger needs before passengers know they need something. Active observation, coupled with anticipation, is the difference between good and great customer service.

Here's another story: I once drove for a well-known A-List Hollywood client who chain-smoked these wacky foreign cigarettes every time she stepped out of the car. One day when I was dropping her off at a meeting, I noticed that she was on her last cigarette. I immediately drove to five different stores and finally found one that stocked the cigarettes. When her meeting was over I asked her:

"Would you like to go get more cigarettes?"

"Do you know any place that sells these?" she said incredulously.

"Sure do—and I stopped and bought you a new pack," I said with a grin.

She was impressed—and her tip was impressive.

What to Say

Your communications fall into two categories: communicating with your coworkers, and communicating with your clients. Your verbal communications with both parties should be respectful and refined. My mother called it "going-to-church talk," which she expected us to use when relatives came over. Your persona should be reflective of the luxury vehicle environment you are in and the type of people you interact with. Your responses should be professional in almost a military style, "Yes sir, no ma'am" manner. Never use first names, and never use street vernacular.

What (and Who) to Know

As a chauffeur, you aren't just expected to drive. You are expected to know everything and anything about your city that a guest may ask you. Your guests are counting on you to make suggestions that could shape their entire visit. Here are just a few of the topics that you need to learn about to be a great chauffeur.

Restaurants

While you don't need to keep a binder, you do need to know your stuff. If a passenger says, "I need to take a client to the best steakhouse around," you should know the name of the best steakhouse, at the bare minimum. An excellent chauffeur will also know the restaurant hours, phone number, and general manager. An excellent chauffeur makes the reservation for the passenger, putting in a word with the manager to ensure star treatment for the passenger.

Every professional chauffeur should know where she is allowed to stage at every major restaurant in her area. Some restaurants let you stay right out front because it is good for business for other patrons to see limousines and fancy cars out front. Other establishments don't have the room and tell chauffeurs they must leave the area after they drop off passengers.

Hotels

This goes for hotels, too. Know the managers, front desk hosts, and all members of the concierge staff. If you have a VIP client you are assigned to for several days, let the hotel staff know that you are willing to make trips to get supplies or take-out for your client. Head parking people at sporting venues and concert venues are also good to know.

Airports

Professional chauffeurs know the layout and particulars of every airport in the area like the inside of their own house. They know where restrooms are; where food store, bars, restaurants and shopping are located; and where the best coffee is. They also know the people who work in the information booths and the counter staff at every airline. They know where page telephones are and how to page passengers from inside the terminal.

The best chauffeurs know which flights come in each day, at each airport they serve, which flights have a history of being late, and how and where to confirm with the local airport traffic controllers the status of each flight. Your company may have a software that tracks flights that you can access to determine when flights will land, but in the end the responsibility of being on time, every time, to pick-up passengers is yours. Familiarize yourself with the flight monitors in the airport and what airport phone number you can call in order to get flight updates. Normally, if you go to the information desk at the airport, staff there will give you the information phone number you can call to request flight statuses.

Know the pick-up/drop-off etiquette for all airports and hotels in your area. There is nothing worse than missing or delaying a passenger because you are parked in the wrong place at the airport or a hotel. There is also nothing more embarrassing for a chauffeur than to have a passenger correct them and direct them to the drop-off location at these locations. You are being paid to know where to park, pick-up and drop off at the airport and know the transportation logistics at every hotel in your area. I have seen even seasoned chauffeurs make novice mistakes that made them and their company look bad and cost them a tip.

I know a chauffeur who took pictures of these signs with his smartphone and sends them to passengers who have never been to the airport, to direct them. At Ambassador, we provided corporate group clients with a PDF by email showing group attendees how to get to baggage claim where our chauffeurs greeted them. Never underestimate a passenger's lack of direction or heightened confusion at a new place. The best chauffeurs I have seen text or call the passenger's cell phone as soon the plane shows landed to inform them specifically where they will meet them.

If you are a new chauffeur, the best way to learn the airport is perform "dry runs" with no passengers and observe where the livery vehicles drop off and pick-up. Then, park your car at each terminal and walk the route your passengers will walk from the airplane gate area (as close as security will allow you) to baggage claim and observe the signs that will direct them to the "limousine" staging area.

Event Pick-up

Sometimes, especially at entertainment and sports venues, the pick-up and drop-off locations are completely different from each other to handle the mass exodus of people and vehicles. You need to be sure your passengers know where to meet you after the show or game so they won't get frustrated and you won't play cell phone tag trying to find each other.

In Tampa, for example, there is one particular sports and concert venue that is a nightmare to get in and out of. The drop-off location is a circle out front that holds 20 cars at a time, which tends to back up into a major thoroughfare if people take too long unloading. At the end of events, police close a road and line up the limousines in three lanes so that if you are not the first car in line you are stuck there until every other party leaves. More times than not, customers get frustrated waiting in this long line that could literally be 15 or 20 cars long.

I worried that my clients would decide this was too long to wait after events and drive themselves to this venue and park in a parking lot. One day I scouted the area and found a law firm across from the venue with an underground parking lot. I went upstairs and asked to speak to one of the principals of the firm. I introduced myself and asked him if we could stage our vehicles in his lot periodically when there were events across the street. We ended up striking a deal whereby I provided him with periodic rides to the airport at no cost. Any time we had passengers going to a concert or game, we used his lot. This expedited the departure from the arena, so my passengers had no wait at all. It became a well-kept secret that Ambassador Limousine was the company to use because we had "special arrangements" and we never got stuck in the throng of vehicles waiting.

I am not saying that in every city across from every venue there is a parking lot to rent. I am saying that you need to look for ways to give your clients what others cannot. Get creative. Know the staff at these venues. Make friends. Don't be afraid to tip someone for a special parking spot.

On night out jobs, the most boring time for chauffeurs is the time they are waiting outside a venue for their passengers to return. While you may be tempted to leave the area and drive around, gas up or go to a convenience store—don't. I guarantee the first time you do will be the time one of your passengers wants to leave early or come back out to the car for something they forgot or just to hang out. If that happens, you look incredibly bad, and more times than not your passengers will get upset. You are being paid to be at their service and wait. Do NOT leave the area. Plan ahead and bring a sandwich with you and a book to read. For goodness' sake, do not sit in the vehicle with the engine off listening to the radio. Because dimes to donuts you will wear down the battery, and when your passengers come out, you won't be able to start the car.

In 2008 the Super Bowl was in Tampa and we had some large contracts and put about 50 extra rented vehicles on the road to service these customers. We had some big-name corporate customers at the game, and I remember getting a frantic call from a part-time chauffeur saying that something was wrong with his SUV, and it would not start. This was about half time and he was upset and did not admit he ran the battery down, so we raced a mechanic out with a spare vehicle to the lot where he was. The mechanic had one hell of a time convincing the lot attendant to let him in, and when he finally did, he got the driver to admit he had been listening to the stereo with the engine off for about 90 minutes. All we needed to do is have the lot attendant call over the tow truck and jump-start the vehicle. The driver made a very novice mistake, but he initially was embarrassed to disclose what he did, so we spent an hour of the mechanic's time, risked not being ready if the passengers came out early, and generally looked like idiots during a very hectic event. Luckily the passengers never found out, but the incident increased our stress level needlessly on one of the most stressful days in the company's history.

While you wait, remember you are still working, and your job is to have your vehicle ready at a moment's notice. When you disembark your passengers initially, re-stage the back of the vehicle, clean the interior, wipe down the windows and surfaces, and keep the vehicle off. Periodically restart it to cool it down and then turn it on with interior lights and climate control set 15 to 20 minutes prior to the time you expect your passengers to be ready for them. Know operating hours, taxi standing locations, phone numbers, and personnel for:

- Concert Venues
- Bars
- Cinemas

What Not to Say

Just as important as what you say is what you don't say. You must always maintain a level of formality, professionalism, and respect. You

Knowledge and Communication

want to be an information portal, not an opinion-giver, so don't let yourself say any of these things.

Cursing: Your verbal communication skills should be appropriate for a professional business environment. Even if you drop the "F" bomb at home, say the word ain't instead of isn't, or use other salty vernacular, this kind of verbal communication is unacceptable as a professional chauffeur.

"I Don't Know": This is the number one thing a chauffeur should not say. It should not be in their vocabulary. If a waiter says "I don't know," I don't think they know what they are doing. Instead, say, "Let me call my office" or "Let me find out for you."

Banned Topics: There are some topics you just should not discuss. Some of them are too sensitive; it is too easy to inadvertently upset someone when talking about these issues. Others are just plain unprofessional to bring up at work. These topics include:

- Politics ("I'm sorry sir/madam, I don't focus too much on politics")
- Sex (a HUGE no-no)
- Religion—don't use the Lord's name in vain (OK it's my parochial school)
- Sports (except to root on the passenger's team)
- Drugs (a BIG no-no)
- Personal life (yours or theirs)

Once during a ride, a chauffeur told me his son died of a heroin overdose. Another chauffeur told me he cheated on his wife. In cases like this, the client feels like an unpaid therapist. In general, you don't want to talk to passengers too much; instead, let them do the talking, and use your listening skills.

What if the passenger tries to talk about something on this list? Work around it. If someone says, "What did you think of that election?" I think of the movie *The Remains of the Day*. In this film, Anthony Hopkins plays Mr. Stevens, the head butler at Darlington Hall. In one scene, a guest at the house asks him about politics. His answer is a polite *"I wouldn't be able to help you with that subject."*

Emulate Mr. Stevens, and do not take a side. Make a general comment such as, "politics/films are not something I follow," and move on. Don't take a side in sports, either; you do not want to offend your passenger. If asked, you can say you are a fan of such-and-such team, but don't insult other teams.

Texting

In 2012, my company provided the majority of the chauffeured transportation for both political conventions for the presidential election. We were hired as the exclusive provider of transportation services by the largest corporate sponsor of both events. We served the Republicans in Tampa, Florida and then packed up 120 vehicles and served the Democrats in Charlotte, North Carolina. One thing we immediately noticed was that the executives we were transporting did not like to answer their cell phones, which caused some logistics issues. It made sense because they were in meetings with politicians and did not want to be interrupted. After the first day, we told chauffeurs not to call passengers when they arrived; they were to simply text them and stand by. Throughout both conventions, texting was the standard operating procedure for every need passengers had. It worked well, and they appreciated the discretion.

When we returned from the conventions, we instituted a

companywide change. When we entered new passenger information, we asked if the passenger received SMS texts on their smartphone and whether they would like our chauffeurs to text them rather than interrupt them with a phone call. We found over 70% of corporate travelers preferred this option. This allowed chauffeurs to be more efficient, and it seems to travelers like a more personal method of serving their needs.

Communication Protocol for Groups and Multi-Stop Trips

Groups, whether corporate clients taking customers out to dinner, professionals going to a convention, or friends enjoying a night out, require extra communication attention. While you will have one main contact person, it is your job to get everyone who started the night in your car safely home or to a hotel. Make sure everyone knows exactly when and where the pick-up will occur. Get every passenger's phone number and do not leave anyone behind. Be ready for changes in plan—don't be surprised if someone decides to go somewhere else for the night or wants to go back to a hotel early.

Confidentiality

What happens in the vehicles stays in the vehicle. My company has many high-profile guests and corporate clients, so we have a strict confidentiality policy. Chauffeurs must keep confidential anything they may observe or hear while driving a guest; chauffeurs even have to sign confidentiality agreements prior to starting work. The only exception is if a guest is engaging in illegal activity or damaging the vehicle.

If a passenger is engaged in personal activity or conversation, pay close attention to your driving. Pretend a partition is up between you and the guest. Some guests will even attempt to test you and see if you are actually listening to their conversations by looking up and asking,

"What do you think about that?" If this happens, always beg their pardon and state, "I'm sorry, I was not listening to your conversation." If they want to further engage you, they will.

If you are driving a celebrity, do not get overly excited and share your location on social media. This could result in a swarm of paparazzi. No matter how tempting it is, do not eavesdrop on the celebrity or tell stories about the celebrity afterwards.

If you are driving business executives, keep confidential any business information you hear. Do not supply any company-specific information; if someone asks, just say the company is "doing well and continuing to grow rapidly." Never give out company or customer names unless you have been given permission to do so. Even if local media mentions that your company has been driving some important people around, do not disclose or confirm client information.

If you are asked by a new corporate customer for references, you can give a general statement such as, "We are the exclusive provider for your hotel and our sports franchise." However, do not tell stories about players or guests. A potential customer will not be impressed if you disclose personal information about your clients. Don't gossip about clients with other drivers, either; in some companies, this could get you fired.

Just Be Quiet and Drive

The biggest mistakes I have seen and the biggest service failures I have witnessed have all been about communication errors. Being professional, keeping the chatter to a minimum, knowing your area, and respecting confidentiality go a long way. If you take this to heart, you'll be better than 90% of chauffeurs.

Things to Master from Chapter Five

- Practice active listening
- Practice actively observing
- Learn what to say
- Learn what to know and where to go
- Learn what never to talk about or say
- When all else fails—keep quiet and drive

CHAPTER SIX

Safe Driving Is Not a Hobby

I am shocked at how little operators train chauffeurs to drive safely or monitor chauffeur driving habits. It seems the majority of companies view safe driving as not having been in an accident this month. In an industry where the biggest customer complaint is poor driving, when livery insurance rates are increasing in double digits annually, and newcomers to the business continually downplay the need for regulation and enhanced driver qualifications, driver safety should be taken very seriously.

Considering that livery vehicles usually traverse double or triple the miles of a typical private car each year, the likelihood a chauffeur will be involved in an accident is also substantially higher.

Customer Complaints About Poor Driving

As soon as I hired my first chauffeur a month into the business, I got my first customer driving complaint. After consulting with many companies in the industry and surveying thousands of customers, I can confirm that the number one complaint of customers who use chauffeured transportation is poor driving.

Each Year in the US there are:	
Passenger Car Accident Deaths	35,000
Non-Fatal Passenger Car Accidents	5,970,000
Passenger car Accidents with Injury	1,700,000
Property-Damage Only Accidents	4,000,000
Number of Reported Accidents:	**6 Million**
Estimated Number of NON-Reported Accidents	3 Million (NTSB)
Total Number of Car Accidents in the U.S.	9 Million (IIFS)

What exactly are chauffeurs doing wrong? At Ambassador Limousine, I email select recent customers a very quick survey and these complaints were the most prevalent:

1) Harsh braking

2) Speeding

3) Changing lanes rapidly without signaling

4) Texting/on the phone/or looking down

Every chauffeur (and every company owner) should query passengers on performance on every trip. For a chauffeur, it is as simple as asking, "Did you find my driving satisfactory today?" right before you depart at the end of each trip. For company owners, I recommend survey cards, survey emails, and follow-up phone calls to passengers every month.

Is it necessary to survey every passenger on every trip? There are a couple of schools of thought on that. Some consumers like the consistency of surveys on every service transaction they partake in. Others get annoyed with them. My advice to operators is to find a non-intrusive, non-threatening way to survey every passenger on every trip one time, for example, by email.

Unbeknownst to my chauffeur and dispatch staff, I used to go on our reservations software and pull a report that gave me a list of passenger emails from trips that week. I simply cut and pasted the names in an email asking them two or three simple questions like:

- Did the chauffeur operate the vehicle safely at all times today?
- Did you completely enjoy your experience?
- On a scale of 1-10 how would you rate our service today?
- If you rate us less than 10, how can we improve?

I always looked at the responses to these emails. I was gratified when someone responded with less than 10 and then took the time to make a suggestion for how we could improve.

Asking passengers these simple questions, whether right at the end of the trip by the chauffeur or by email the next day, confirms that they are happy with the customer service experience they are paying for. Knowing this data is critical to future revenue generation of each chauffeur and the growth of your company. Do not ignore or dismiss customers who complain.

Here are some important facts about consumers who complain about poor service experiences:

a) 85% are complaining because they want to use your services again.

b) Generally, businesses hear from only 4% of customers who are dissatisfied.

c) For every person who complains, 26 remain silent.

d) News of a bad customer experience gets to three times as many people as news of a great customer experience.

Recently I had a company owner participant in a seminar on this subject approach me.

"How do you know poor driving is unsafe?" he asked. "I get those complaints from customers every once in a while, but none of my drivers have been in an accident or gotten speeding tickets in my cars."

After I picked myself up off the floor, I explained to the group that the service we are being paid a premium to provide is not simply giving someone a ride from point A to point B. It is delivering the passenger in a safe and enjoyable manner. If a customer takes the time to mention that the chauffeur is driving poorly, I think it is OK to assume they mean the chauffeur was driving in a manner that the passenger felt was less than safe. Even if you have not gotten in any accidents or been cited for speeding tickets or driving infractions, you are not automatically a safe driver.

When we hired new chauffeurs, we pull their MVDR (Motor Vehicle Driving Record). In some states these reports may be called something else, but basically it is a record from the Motor Vehicle Bureau (DMV in some states) that shows whether your license is valid; any vehicle registered in your name; and driving infractions like DUI, reckless driving, speeding tickets, or any moving violations received from law enforcement over a given period of time. Most states keep 36 to 60 months of driving data on everyone in their state with an operator's license.

As a company policy, we hired only chauffeurs who were completely free of moving violations for the past 36 months and remained free of violations while employed.

I was surprised by the complaints we received from customers about poor driving when chauffeurs had perfect MVDR's. To me, this was clear evidence that just because you were not in an accident or caught driving badly does not mean you are necessarily a safe driver. It taught me that heretofore, you have just been lucky.

I know a lot of people who are terrible drivers. They have not been caught speeding or experienced accidents, but I would not trust them to drive passengers for a living.

What Causes Accidents?

How do accidents happen in the first place? Here are the top ten reasons.

1. Speeding: The term "speed demon" exists for a reason. You already know how much more time it takes to brake when you are going fast, so it stands to reason that when you go really fast, you are far more likely to crash.

2. Reckless Driving: Trying to emulate something you saw in an action movie or a video game generally counts as reckless driving. Going way above the speed limit, swerving, making sudden movements without signaling, and other risky choices could be detrimental to you, your passengers, and others on the road. And, unlike in a video game, there isn't another life waiting for you after you crash. A major form of reckless driving is failure to yield the right of way, including running red lights and stop signs.

3. Cell Phone Use: There's a reason why so many cities and states have outlawed cell phone use while driving. If you need to use your phone to check in with dispatch, check in when you first get in the vehicle with passengers and the vehicle is still in park. Then, put the phone down and start driving.

4. Other Forms of Distracted Driving: Sure, you may know not to check your email while driving. But what about reaching over to get your sunglasses? Changing the radio station? Chatting with your passengers? Having a snack? The truth is, these things result in many accidents each day.

5. Driver Fatigue: Falling asleep behind the wheel is a very real danger, as tired commuters, truck drivers, and sleep-deprived parents can attest. Avoid taking an unplanned nap in the driver's seat by always coming to your job well rested.

6. Driving Under the Influence: You don't need me to tell you that driving under the influence of alcohol or other drugs is one of the most dangerous things you can do. Driving after a few drinks can raise your likelihood of causing an accident exponentially.

7. Rubbernecking: "Look at that gorgeous sunset!" your passenger says to you. But you know better! Rubbernecking is another type of distracted driving and takes place when drivers look other things on the road not linked to their driving. Accidents, sunsets, and billboards can all be interesting, but you have to keep your eyes on the road.

8. Defective Automobile and Automobile Parts: Tire, seatbelt, airbag, and other vehicle defects can put you and your passengers in danger. Thorough inspections can help minimize this danger.

9. Poor Weather Conditions: Icy roads, high winds, rain, and other environmental factors can make driving much more dangerous. If driving conditions deteriorate, pay extra attention and slow down. If you are going the speed limit during a whiteout, you are going too fast.

10. Construction Zones: If you hit a construction zone, slow down! Construction zones often contain debris, cones, and other roadblocks that could cause an accident, not to mention actual construction workers walking in and out of the road.

How to Be a Safe Driver

Whether you realize it or not, more times than not the passenger is watching you drive making mental notes about how you perform. Make safe driving a habit, and regardless of how many years you have driven, or how many years it has been since you had an accident, learn and practice these techniques. Remember, first and foremost you are a silent sentry of safety, making sure your passengers arrive at their destination without incident.

Commit and Concentrate

Being a safe driver part of the time is like being half pregnant. It can't be done. You are either a safe driver with safe driving habits, or you are not. So as a professional chauffeur, the best way to hone your safe driving skills is to always practice safe driving in your livery vehicle and your personal vehicle.

Know Your Vehicle

Safe driving starts with knowing the vehicle you are driving. That means knowing all the functions and features of the vehicle and knowing that everything works properly as designed before you start out for the day. Knowing your vehicle and all safety features ensures a comfortable ride and proper actions in the event of a near or actual accident.

When they are assigned the vehicle for the first time, a professional chauffeur takes the time to learn about the vehicle by reviewing the operator's manual. Then they perform the walk around and function check at the beginning of every shift. The pre-drive inspection is paramount. Inspect the interior, exterior, and trunk. Check that the tires have good tread, windshield wipers work, the spare tire is inflated, emergency kit is in the trunk, and the windshield washer fluid receptacle is filled. Test the lights (hazards, blinkers, highbeams, and brake lights). Make sure brakes and emergency brakes are functioning. Make sure the vehicle is shifting is smoothly and seat belt harnesses are functioning. Finally, ensure that there are no warning lights on the dashboard.

Exercise Proper Driving Technique

Remember when you took Driver's Education in high school? They make have they emphasized keeping your hands at "10 and 2" on the steering wheel. Then why do so many drivers you observe daily drive with one hand on the wheel and the other in their lap, clutching their cell phone, or elbow resting comfortably on the doorsill? As a professional chauffeur, you are onstage when you drive. Be aware of where your hands are at all times. Yes, they should be firmly on the steering wheel in the 10 o'clock and 2 o'clock positions. Get in the habit of having your hands at the 10 o' clock and 2 o'clock positions on the steering wheel while facing straight ahead at all times.

Above and beyond hand position on the steering wheel, safe driving with passengers in the car includes monitoring your speed, monitoring dashboard instruments, knowing what vehicles surround you at all times, and knowing that your passengers are comfortable and safe in your charge. In short, you must be totally aware of your surroundings, your vehicle, and what is going on with both.

In a prior career I trained bodyguards and stood post myself performing executive protection services and we used an observation technique when guarding a subject called 12, 3, 6, 9 (using a clock face as a guide). This technique allows protective agents to observe everything in their field of view very methodically. It is also a great way to observe what is around your vehicle to help you drive safely. This routine takes seconds and will become a natural habit anytime you drive. You don't need to move your head to do it; you only need to move your eyes.

- 12: Look directly in front of you (where the car is headed).

- 3: Look to the passenger side, checking the side of the vehicle and the passenger door rear view mirror.

- 6: Glance at the windshield rear view mirror check on the passenger and traffic at the back of the car.

- 9: Finally, look at the side mirror on the driver's door and the traffic on that side of the vehicle.

In all cases, your head movements while driving should be minimal, and your hands should stay properly positioned on the wheel. This is why I recommend asking the passenger about the climate, radio stations, and amenities like spring water before you put the vehicle in drive.

Defensive Driving

You must be ready for anything that could occur while you are driving and practice defensive driving. What is defensive driving? It is a set of driving skills that when practiced and used daily allow you to defend yourself against possible collisions caused by bad drivers, drunk drivers, and poor weather. If you look ahead and keep your eyes scanning around your vehicle in the fashion described above, you spot potential hazards more easily.

Once you have identified a potential hazard and decided what to do, act immediately. Defensive drivers are able to avoid dangers on the road and reduce their chances of an accident by using these safe driving practices.

Tips for defensive driving:

a) Plan ahead for the unexpected by knowing what is well in front of your vehicle and surrounding your vehicle at all times.

Safe Driving Is Not a Hobby

b) Control your speed at all times.

c) Be prepared to react to other drivers—all drivers, the young and the old.

d) Do not expect the other drivers to do what you think they should do.

e) Respect others on the roadway—all others; truckers, construction crews, etc.

f) Be aware of driving in special conditions like traffic congestion, construction zones, or poor weather conditions.

g) Keep a safe distance between you and vehicles in front of you.

Slow Speed Accidents

According to annual data by the National Highway Traffic Safety Administration, 50% of all accident fatalities occur when your vehicle is going between 30 and 40 miles per hour. Remember, you may be going 25 miles per hour, but the guy that went through the stop sign might be going 45 miles per hour.

Leaving enough room between you and the next vehicle to anticipate the need for quick braking in the event of an emergency can mean the difference between an accident or near accident. Rear-end collisions account for 30% of all accidents and a significant number of injuries and fatalities. The difference between an actual rear-end collision and near collision in driver response time can be as little as half a second.

The biggest factor in stopping distances is the speed at which a driver reacts to seeing the hazard. Even seasoned drivers take between one and three seconds, and older drivers take even longer.

At 35 miles per hour you are traveling at 51 feet per second.

Driving Your Income

At 70 mph you are traveling 103 feet PER SECOND, so a half second reaction time can potentially be the difference between life and death. Consider the following stopping time table based on traveling at certain speeds.

STOPPING DISTANCES FOR DRY PAVEMENT/ROAD[21]

Speed	Thinking Distance 2	Braking Distance	Overall Stopping Distance	Comparisons
20 MPH	20 FEET	20 feet	40 feet	
30 MPH	30 FEET	45 feet	75 feet	Full length of tractor/semi-trailer
40 MPH	40 FEET	80 feet	120 feet	
50 MPH	50 FEET	125 feet	175 feet	
60 MPH	60 FEET	180 feet	240 feet	
70 MPH	70 FEET	245 feet	315 feet	(USA = "Touchdown!")
80 MPH	80 FEET	320 feet	400 feet	About **six** semi-trailer lengths

(SOURCE- DRIVE AND STAY ALIVE, INC.)

---

[21] Driveandstayalive.com

STOPPING DISTANCES FOR WET PAVEMENT/ROAD [22]

Speed	Thinking Distance [2]	Possible Braking Distance	Overall Stopping Distance Can Be:	Comparisons
20 mph	20 FEET	40 feet	60 feet	
30 MPH	30 FEET	90 feet	120 feet	
40 MPH	40 FEET	160 feet	200 feet	
50 MPH	50 FEET	250 feet	300 feet	*(USA = Touchdown !)*
60 MPH	60 FEET	360 feet	420 feet	
70 MPH	70 FEET	490 feet	560 feet	
80 MPH	80 FEET	640 feet	720 feet	Almost two and a half Football fields [3]

(SOURCE: DRIVE AND STAY ALIVE, INC.)

When the road is icy or covered with compacted snow, the braking distance for your vehicle can be as much as *ten times* further than for dry roads/pavement.

At higher speeds, braking takes much longer. If you double your speed—say from 30 mph to 60 mph—your braking distance does not

---

22 Driveandstayalive.com

become twice as long; it becomes *four times* as long.

Want to estimate more stopping distances? To convert miles per hour (MPH) to feet per second (FPS) the easy way, divide MPH traveled by 2, then multiply by 3. Your answer will be accurate plus/minus 5%. As an example, 100 miles per hour converts to 150 feet per second. The true answer, when done with a longer calculation, is 147 feet per second.

Always Leave a Three-Second Gap

If you are on a dry, clear road and you reach the same fixed point before you can say "three-Mississippi," then you are too close to the vehicle in front of you. To create a three-second gap between you and the vehicle in front of you, look at an object like a street light, telephone pole, or building on the side of the road. Count "One Mississippi, two Mississippi, three Mississippi" to create the essential minimum of *a three-second gap*.

Thanks to better brake technology, stopping distances have reduced somewhat over the years. However, it has to be remembered that, no matter how good the brakes and tires, the laws of physics don't change.

Slippery Roads Anti-Lock Braking System (ABS)

You probably learned about Anti-Lock Braking Systems, or ABS, in driving school as well. Before ABS, when drivers slammed on the brakes, their brakes would lock, and they would be likely to skid or slip off of the road. ABS pumps the brakes more rapidly than any human could, maintaining braking power and keeping the brakes from locking even on a slippery road. If you feel your ABS kick on, keep your foot firmly on the brake, and steer the vehicle to avoid a collision.

Seat Belts and Airbags: A Winning Combination

According to NHTSA, seat belts save\ more than 100,000 lives annually. As a professional chauffeur, you set the tone for safety on each ride. So buckle up, and insist your passengers do also.

It's important for everyone in a moving vehicle to wear seat belts. These restraints keep your body in the car, and in a position that allows the airbag to cushion your impact.

Airbags certainly make cars safer, but they're designed to work in conjunction with seat belts, which help prevent passenger ejection during high-speed crashes and rollovers. However, airbags can be dangerous if passengers don't first use safety belts. Airbags deploy with incredible force, enough to cause injury to passengers not wearing seat belts.

Kids and Car Seats

If you've ever wondered why children always seem to be in the back of the vehicle, the airbag is a big part of the answer. Front-seat airbags are designed with an adult's height and needs in mind. The force of a deploying airbag can hit a child in the wrong spot, leading to injury or even death. The same can be said for an infant, even if she or he is in a rear-facing infant seat. The force of the airbag can go through the seat and injure or kill a child.

In the US, car crashes are the leading cause of death for children. Here are a few safety tips to make sure children stay safe under your watch:

- Have children under 13 sit in the back seat.
- Place children in car seats or booster seats appropriate to their weights and heights.

- If having an older child in the front seat cannot be avoided, move the seat as far back as possible, and make sure the child's seatbelt is properly fastened.

- Do not use car seats that were in car accidents (they may be defective).

It is imperative that you know your company's policy on car seats and follow it. We used to supply car seats and booster seats because believe it or not, parents failed to tell us when they were traveling with small children and showed up at the airport with toddlers and no seat. If your company does not have a policy on this, I suggest you urge them to create one.

Don't Break the Eggs

You may recall that I used to test my chauffer's driving skills by telling them to pretend there is a flat dish containing a dozen eggs in the back seat. Pretending that there is a glass of champagne in the back seat works, too. Test your own driving skills by pretending that there is a glass of champagne duct taped to the back seat. Would it spill under your watch? With certain guests, there may actually be a glass of champagne in the back seat, and you can bet your guest will be disappointed if your driving causes a spill. By sharpening your driving skills, you can keep your guests, their children, and even their beverages safe from harm.

Things to Master from Chapter Six:

- #1 complaint of customers: poor driving.

- Learn what causes accidents so you can avoid them.

- Learn how to be a safe driver.

- Practice defensive driving.
- Practice safe stopping distance—leave a 3-second gap.
- Know your company policy on car seats.
- Smooth driving equals more tips and fewer complaints.

CHAPTER SEVEN

When Something Goes Wrong (and it will!)

We are in a business with many moving parts. Inevitably, you will be the chauffeur on a trip where something goes wrong and impacts the customer experience. Knowing this, the professional chauffeur has a plan of what to say and what to do to when something negative happens on a trip.

What to Do When Something Goes Wrong

If something happens on a trip that detracts from the customer's experience, you have to main goals: minimize the damage to the customer's experience and salvage the long-term customer relationship. This troubleshooting plan ensures that you do the best job possible when the wheels, metaphorically, fall off the bus.

1) Speak to the passenger directly and ensure that you understand the issue. Recite the issue back to the customer so they know you understand. Ask open-ended questions until you fully understand the issue.

2) Write down what happened and what the passenger said so you won't forget important details. The written documentation will be useful later.

3) Take ownership of the passenger's issue. Act as if you are the one responsible for the problem, even if you did not cause it. Apologize to the passenger, assure them that this type of issue is rare, and tell him that you are going to take whatever steps need to resolve the issue.

4) Provide the passenger with your plan of action and an estimated time they will hear back from someone concerning the issue.

5) Ask management to contact the passenger to make sure the passenger is comfortable with the resolution. By making direct contact with the passenger, management ensures that all is well. This follow-up call also gives the passenger a good impression of your company.

6) If the issue that occurred was very negative to the customer experience, ask management to surprise the passenger with a gift or perk, such as a gift card or a 25 percent discount on her next purchase. This gesture tells the customer that his patronage is appreciated.

What Could Go Wrong?

In this business, I've seen the same problems occur over and over. They tend to fall under these categories.

Late Arrival or Departures

Late arrivals happen for a variety of reasons. Sometimes, dispatch may cut it close and not give you adequate time to get to the customer. At other times, traffic may impede you from being on time. In some cases, the chauffeur makes a mistake and shows up late.

Avoid It: Communicate adequately with customers and dispatch to make sure you have the right arrival times. Always give yourself plenty of time to pick-up passengers: as a rule in the industry, we get to pick-up locations 15 minutes before the scheduled pick-up time. If you are going to be late, let both parties know immediately.

Missing Special Instructions

Some guests make special requests when making reservations. For example, a guest might have dogs that bark at anyone who pulls into the driveway; she may ask that the chauffeur park on the street to avoid startling the dogs. Regular guests often have recurring special requests, such as a certain newspaper to read or a favorite beverage to drink.

Avoid missing instructions: When dispatch and the chauffeur fail to communicate and inadvertently ignore these requests, guests are understandably peeved. Always double-check with dispatch about special requests. If a customer has requested a specific item, allot yourself time to go get it.

Traffic

Getting stuck in traffic can make even the most tranquil chauffeurs mad. Luckily, this is usually easy to avoid.

Avoid It: Know alternate routes to every destination, and keep traffic patterns in mind. For example, Route 93 going into Boston is always backed up in the morning. If you get on Route 93 at 8:00 a.m. expecting to get somewhere quickly, that's your fault. Similarly, familiarize yourself with events (sports games, political events, etc.) that cause traffic and avoid those areas if you can.

Crabby Passengers

Have you ever met someone who is impossible to please? Once in a while, you will encounter these people on the job. Some passengers seem like they won't be happy unless you bring them caviar on a gold platter, which you probably aren't in a position to do. I once had a passive-aggressive who would not complain directly to the chauffeur. Instead, she had her assistant call to complain about the chauffeur the day after the ride.

Deal With It: There is no way to avoid crabby passengers, just like there is no way to avoid crabby people in everyday life. It can require self-control, but if you have a crabby passenger, don't get confrontational and take the blame for everything. Follow your When Something Goes Wrong protocol and tell management.

If the crabby passenger is also a regular client, letting management know about complaints is even more important. Only 8% of US residents use chauffeuring services, and it is important that chauffeuring companies don't lose any of their hard-won customers. Management can meet with perpetually unsatisfied clients to try and assure them that they are important and address their complaints.

Extreme Weather

Mother Nature is a fickle mistress. Unsafe conditions, such as snowstorms, thunderstorms, and the like can adversely affect the customer experience.

Deal With It: Pay attention to the weather, especially if your guest is headed to the airport. If you suspect that the passenger's flight might be delayed, check with the airport immediately and adjust the trip accordingly. Additionally, pay extra attention to driving safely in inclement weather.

Mechanical Failure

Imagine that you are waiting for a passenger, parked at the curb, and suddenly you hear your engine sputter and die. What now?

Avoid It: Check your car carefully every time you pick it up. If, while in between trips, you suspect something is wrong, park and request a new car. If you drive your own car, end your shift early and take your car to a mechanic. A mechanical failure could be dangerous for you and your clients; it is better to address it immediately than to ignore it and suffer the consequences.

Deal With It: After ensuring that your guest is unhurt, call your office and request another car to come for the passenger. If there is not one available, call another company and ask them to send a car. Your passenger should not be late to an appointment or miss a flight because your car died. Your office will likely arrange for a tow truck to come for the vehicle. Document what happened, along with any observation (weird noises, smells) to help the mechanic figure out what's wrong.

ACCIDENTS

An accident is the worst possible thing that can go wrong while you are driving a passenger. Don't make it worse by panicking or handling it badly. If an accident occurs, your goals are to a) make sure the passenger is safe, b) get alternative transportation, and c) avoid litigation. Stick to protocol and the passenger may be impressed by your professionalism rather than incensed.

Accident Protocol

1) Make sure your client is OK. Call an ambulance if there is any hint of injury; better safe than sorry. If the passenger is unhurt, get them off to the side and in a safe place.

2) **Check out the vehicle.** See if it is OK to drive.

3) **Call the office and the police.** Even if the accident seems very minor, your office needs a police report for insurance reasons. Call the office first and explain exactly what happened. The office may call police, or they may ask you to do so.

Often, other drivers assume that chauffeuring services have excellent insurance and try to get thousands of dollars in accident claims, even if the car is fine. One time, one of my chauffeurs tapped a woman's bumper. No one was hurt, and they didn't take any pictures or call the police. The woman's husband called the next day, yelling about lots of damage under the bumper. He wanted over a thousand dollars to replace the bumper.

An accident report helps chauffeuring services avoid this situation. Get a name, badge number, and a business card from the police officer to make follow-up easier. When talking to police and other drivers, do not admit fault, even if the accident was your fault.

4) **Get alternate transportation for your client.** The office will send another car for the client. If there is no other car available, ask if you can call a competitor to request another car at your company's expense.

5) **Use your accident kit.** It will likely include a disposable camera and an accident form with a diagram. No matter how minor the accident seems, record everything from the other driver (license, registration, damage, etc.) just in case. Use your smartphone to take pictures or even video.

Keep Your Cool

No business is perfect. Due to circumstances within or out of your control, you will eventually find yourself with an irate passenger or a malfunctioning vehicle. Doing everything you can to avoid these situations, and handling them gracefully when they do occur, is what separates an average chauffeur from a great professional chauffeur.

Things to Master from Chapter Seven:

- Learn what to do when something goes wrong (and it will).
- Be prepared by knowing what commonly goes wrong in our business.
- Learn your company's accident protocol.

CHAPTER EIGHT

Meet the Passenger

Only between 8% to 10% of the population of the United States use chauffeured black car or limousine services on a routine basis. A bit over 15% use taxis annually, and most taxi users are in bigger cities like New York and Chicago.[23]

The most frequent users of chauffeured transportation are people who live or work within 30 to 40 miles of an urban area with an international airport. They are typically top-earning business owners or executives, affluent individuals, or couples between the ages of 35 and 65 (Generation X-er's and slightly older). These are people who are well established; they own a home and their house value is in the top 20% for houses in a given area. They may have a C-level executive position in business, like Chief Executive Officer, or have a profession with advanced education like a doctor, lawyer, accountant, or financial planner.

Our customers purchase luxury vehicles, frequently dine at fine restaurants, shop at premium stores, take annual vacations, and in general enjoy the finer things in life. They are frequent flyers for business or pleasure, and when they travel, they stay at finer hotels. These consumers view chauffeured transportation as a convenience and a lifestyle choice over other modes of transportation during specific events like trips to the airport, sporting events, concerts, or nights out.

---

23   The Changing Face of Taxi and Limousine Drivers, Schaller Consulting

TNCs like Uber, Lyft, and the Changing Customer Personas

Since TNCs like Uber and Lyft arrived on the scene, the number of frequent passengers of chauffeured transportation services is growing by 5% per month by some estimates.[24] The APP. technology is increasing the number of people utilizing (non-taxi) chauffeured transportation by well over 50% annually. Additionally, the age and income strata of this new frequent passenger in urban areas is shifting to the 20 to 30-something Gen Y crowd, with a lower income than traditional chauffeured transportation users.

There is also a crossover segment of the population that use both traditional chauffeured transportation and now have become user *"advocates"* of TNCs based on being "early adopters" of the smartphone technology application that eases ordering service. The crossover segment uses TNCs in big cities they frequently travel in as a replacement for metered cabs and reserved black cars from the airport[25]. At the same time, they may still reserve luxury transportation from their home to the airport, so be aware of these dual users and never speak badly about TNCs—or any other competitor, for that matter.

Corporate Travelers

Corporate Travelers use Chauffeured Transportation for a number of reasons. Corporate travelers who fly domestically and internationally account for as much as 45% of the total revenue of small-to-medium-sized livery companies (who have fleets of between 1 to 20 vehicles) to over 85% of several of the top ten chauffeured transportation firms in the US (100-plus-vehicle fleets).[26] Individual corporate travelers use livery services primarily to get to and from airports as well as in each city for business events and evenings out.

---

24   Wall Street Journal – TNC technology firms
25   See previous
26   LCT Magazine Fact Book 2016

Corporate travelers value service, safety, and professionalism rather than a low price. According to a survey of over 120 corporate travel buyers, price rated fifth in overall importance, taking a backseat to complaint resolution, insurance for drivers, ease of making bookings, and licensing of drivers. Flexibility in negotiating transient pricing ranked even lower, though that attribute also scored lowest of all attributes in terms of buyer satisfaction. A recurring theme in buyer open-ended responses was the need for "reliable, safe and impeccable" service, particularly as company VIPs tended to be the ones who used the services most often.[27]

One corporate executive trip may be the floodgate to hundreds of future trips and sizeable revenue. If it goes well, you cement the relationship for another trip. If it goes poorly, your trip may lose your company a valuable customer. So, you must be on your A Game (remember Service DNA) for these trips.

Providing Quality Service to Corporate Travelers:

a) *Know the pick-up, drop off, wait locations, baggage claim, and restrooms at every international airport in the service area.*

b) *Know the procedures for picking up at every FBO or Fixed Base Operation (private executive hangars) in the service area.*

c) *Know where every hotel is in the service areas and knows where to drop off, park, and wait.*

d) *Know where every high-end restaurant is for corporate entertaining.*

e) *Know how to traverse the entire geographic service area, specifically business parks, high-rises, and commerce cent*ers.

---

27 *Business Travel News 2017*

Airport Service for Corporate Travelers

Corporate travelers use chauffeured transportation to go to and from the airport from their home, office, or hotels. Many business executives use chauffeured transportation to the airport when they fly for convenience, safety, efficiency, and enjoyment. For some it is a business perk that their company pays for. Frequent travelers prefer chauffeured transportation over driving themselves to the airport or taking a communal "shuttle" to minimize stress and to eliminate the need to leave an expensive personal vehicle at the airport, avoiding damage to their vehicle and excessive onsite parking charges.

Corporate travelers can be demanding and are certainly some of the most discriminating customers of chauffeured transportation. Because these passengers experience chauffeured services often and in different geographic areas, they know good service and bad service. The individual corporate traveler is first and foremost concerned about guaranteed punctual service. The last thing a corporate traveler wants is a no-show or late vehicle. They may miss their flight, and that could cost hundreds even thousands in extra travel expenses and lost revenue. If this were to occur, they have been known to call the executive assistant who made the reservation or email the corporate travel department and request never to be booked with the offending company again.

A professional chauffeur can impress corporate travelers by being on their A Game. Corporate travelers are usually in a rush to get from place to place, and air travel is especially hectic and tiring. While they are in your charge, you should consider yourself their personal assistant and anticipate their needs. Maybe they are hungry, tired, thirsty, or want to relax and listen to jazz, read a magazine, or borrow a pack of mints for their next meeting. If the trip is long, maybe they would like to take their shoes off and rest their feet.

Meet the Passenger

Smartphones and Texting

The smartphone is the best way I know for today's chauffeur to impress their passengers with current information. The best professional chauffeur I know provides corporate traveler with information they need to ensure a successful trip and ease their anxiety. If he is transporting the passenger to the airport for a flight, he verifies whether the passenger's plane is on time or delayed while he waits and tells the passenger during the greeting. He checks the news in the arrival city, including the sports teams playing, and let the passenger know what is going on. He also verifies the weather in the destination city for the next three days and lets the passenger know what they can expect.

Speaking of smartphones, remember that corporate travelers, in particular, prefer to be texted rather than called (it is impossible to answer a phone call in a meeting). Many professional chauffeurs text their next passenger while en route and ask them if they want something special to eat or drink that can be picked up on the way. Here's an example text:

"Mr. Smith, there is a Starbucks on the way to your hotel. Can I stop and get something for you before I come get you?"

To do this, first you must know the area and secondly you must have the time in between trips. You could also carry drinks and snacks in your supplies. I have seen some chauffeurs put together a frequent traveler kit that includes things like gum, mints, and even foam earplugs that guests can take with them. The best chauffeurs go the extra mile PRIOR to picking up the customer by, for example, picking up the newspaper from the passenger's hometown or picking up a favorite coffee for a regular passenger, etc.

Corporate Entertaining

Corporate travelers may require transportation to and from the office, hotel, or home for evenings out. When corporate executives want to create stronger relationships with clients or potential clients, they usually take them out to dinner at a fine restaurant or out to a professional sporting event or concert. When alcohol is being served, prudent business professionals rely on chauffeured transportation to and from these types of events. Even if they may be meeting their client at the venue, in many cases the corporate executive will reserve chauffeured transportation for themselves if alcohol is being served.

In these cases, the professional chauffeur must follow the direction of the passengers and communicate with them throughout the entire evening to ensure proper service.

Find Out Who's In Charge: Establish who the person in charge is for the evening—this is the key passenger you will establish logistics with. Please don't assume it is the CEO. She is there to entertain clients and do business; as such; she may designate all the transportation coordination to an underling. If she refers you to another person in the group, you are to communicate and discuss logistics with that individual and not the boss. Simply ask your dispatcher whom you should expect to coordinate with, or address this with the group itself at the beginning of the evening and establish whom you will be coordinating with. This does not mean you will not talk to the rest of the group; it is to identify whom you will discuss logistics and establish locations and times with. This sets the expectations for the evening.

Establish a Pick-Up Location and Time: Coordinate the exact pick-up location and times with the passengers, and do not leave it to chance that the passenger will see you parked across the street. If you are transporting two or three people, coordinating everything is usually an easy task. As the number of passengers increases, so does the need to communicate final logistic decisions with all of them. Once you establish a pick-up location at the venue for the ride home with the key passenger in charge, make sure all guests know the location and time. If you have a larger group, write down names and cell numbers. It is your responsibility to ensure that everyone is back in your vehicle to go home.

Protect Possessions: Always offer to lock personal possessions of the guests in the trunk before they disembark at the venue. (Make sure the trunk is impeccably clean prior to starting out.)

Re-stage: After you have dropped off your guests for dinner or for the start of the game always clean and re-stage your vehicle. Do not wait until closer to the pick-up at the end of the event in case clients need an unplanned ride, want to leave early, or part of the group wants to come down and simply sit in the vehicle to wait for the others. Never assume you have time to clean the vehicle later. As soon as you drop off passengers at the beginning of the night, prepare your vehicle for the return trip.

Corporate Group Transportation

Group transportation usually means transporting attendees of conferences, conventions or corporate meetings to and from airports to hotels and/or corporate offices. Most corporate groups require special operational logistics planning for both dispatchers and professional chauffeurs assigned to the group. Group transportation also includes transporting larger groups in large-capacity vehicles to planned events around the host city.

The keys to being a top-quality corporate group transportation chauffeur are professionalism, punctuality, and communication. In many cases, group attendees may be at this particular airport for the first time and don't know where to go to meet their ride. It is also imperative that chauffeurs communicate with dispatchers, bookers, greeters, or staffers when passengers arrive and if particular passengers have special requests.

We are trained to meet or exceed every passenger's expectations and never, ever say no. In the case of corporate groups, this absolutely applies. However, it is always advisable to clear special requests with dispatchers, bookers, or the group leader before saying yes to the individual passenger. For example, if a group passenger wants to stop on the way to the hotel at a pharmacy or store, ask the group leader or dispatch before stopping. You don't want to overly accommodate one passenger and make your next passengers from the same group wait at the airport because you made an unapproved stop.

ALL-DAY CORPORATE TRANSPORTATION

> ***Road Show***: *A presentation by an issuer of securities to potential buyers.* ***Road shows*** *refer to when the management of a* ***company*** *that is issuing securities or doing an initial public offering (IPO) travels around the country to give presentations to analysts, fund managers and potential investors.*

Road show corporate transportation usually involves multiple stops during several hours or full days, going to meetings your corporate customers may have around a city. The day of travel is usually critical to the success of their future endeavors. For example, your clients may be launching a product and meeting with prospective investors to raise capital.

On multi-vehicle charters and corporate groups, it is a good idea to designate one seasoned chauffeur that all other chauffeurs will follow. This will be the lead person to communicate with the group leader and the office. This helps to reduce miscommunications and tends to keep vehicles and passengers better organized.

During road shows, be knowledgeable, accommodating, patient, and flexible. You must know precisely how to transport your passengers to multiple destinations throughout your time together with no mistakes or mishaps. The timetable for this day of travel is very precise, and meeting times are usually set in stone. It is your job to get them from place to place on time. Typically, these passengers are focused on a high-stakes agenda, and they need your help. Whenever you can anticipate their needs and accommodate them, it is appreciated. Stock your vehicle with extra mints and beverages, and ask in advance if there is anything that you can do to make their day a success.

Affiliate or "Network" Passengers

An affiliate is another chauffeured transportation company in another city that provides service to passengers in their area and facilitates service in any other city the traveler goes to. These passengers usually communicate with them directly, and that company communicates with your company to reserve a vehicle. This eliminates the need for the passenger or their staff having to find companies around the country (and the world, in many cases) to chauffeur them in strange cities. It also eliminates the need for them to provide credit card and billing information to multiple companies.

A national network is a company that specializes in servicing the worldwide transportation needs of corporate travelers by vetting several qualified chauffeured transportation companies in each market around the world. The largest national network companies are based in large cities like Boston, New York, Chicago, DC, and Los Angeles, where large corporations are based. Many network companies have fleets in several cities and contract with small to medium-sized firms in other cities.

Special Considerations for Affiliate and Network Passengers

Affiliate and network passengers expect flawless service, as do the companies they book with. The professional chauffeur knows to be especially attentive to these passengers and follow all the specific instructions your company has for them. These passengers expect the same things your regular clients expect: punctuality, professionalism, and safe driving.

Networks and affiliates do not want you to provide their passengers with any material or communications that has your primary company name on it. You are not representing your primary company; you are representing the affiliate. Never give these passengers your business card, and never tell them to call your company directly. If they ask you whom you work for, say you are part of the XYZ national network.

Affiliate and network companies go to great lengths to preserve and enhance the relationship they have with their customers, so every trip you provide for these companies will be scrutinized. These companies often survey passengers and take inspection trips to make sure chauffeurs are adhering to protocol. Several network companies fly in employees to ride in your vehicle as if they are a retail passenger, to evaluate chauffeurs.

LEISURE PASSENGERS

Who They Are

Night-out passengers spend disposable income on chauffeured transportation as part of their enjoyment and or entertainment. They work hard by day and want to relax and unwind at night. Many of them have high-paying careers and they recognize that if they drink to excess, drive their own vehicle, they are risking a career-ending DUI.

However, a bad experience could convince them to spend those dollars on other forms of enjoyment or entertainment, so you must be on your toes when transporting them.

Customers who regularly use chauffeured transportation services for night- out leisure activities are some of the most desirable passengers a professional chauffeur can have. These passengers often "spoil with service," so that on their next occasion out they will request you as their chauffeur. These customers need a car for the whole night, and thus the bill at the end of the night is in multiple hundreds of dollars and the gratuity higher due to the multi-hours of use. So, providing these customers with exceptional service is exceptionally important.

What They Expect

Usually leisure passengers are heading to a concert, professional sporting event, an elegant restaurant, charity event, or other entertainment venue when they reserve a limousine for the entire evening. Many times, they are going to multiple locations during the evening. If your company is in an area with lots of local landmarks like New York, Hollywood, or Washington DC, perhaps they want to take a city tour. Regardless of where your client is heading, there is usually a schedule of stops for the evening. Sometimes there will be multiple pick-up locations because clients invite their friends along, so knowing this well in advance of the start is critical. This is where the pre-trip phone call to the client is very valuable.

Planning: The most important part of your job is getting these passengers to their events on time. The last thing you want is to make your clients late for their concert, dinner reservations, or the first pitch because you did not time the ride correctly. The customer is counting on you as the professional to get them to their event on time. If you are taking them to a game or concert, they expect you to know how much traffic will be around the venue. They expect you to know the traffic volume on the highways at that particular time. Knowing this and planning properly will have a great impact on your tip.

Prior to every night-out assignment, I suggest calling the passenger (or their executive assistant) to get details either the day of or day before the event. Introduce yourself to the customer and ask them if you can get anything special beside ice and water for the evening. Ask if you are picking anyone else up and asked what time they wished to arrive at the venue or restaurant. Right then on the phone I could usually tell them if the proposed pick-up time made sense or offered a suggestion of a slightly earlier pick-up so we would not arrive late at their destination. I can't tell you how many concerts we would have rolled up to 30 minutes late if I followed their initial pick-up times. Make your recommendations; you transport passengers for a living, so your suggestions will usually be listened to.

Amenities: As soon as your passengers are in the vehicle, familiarize them with the amenities and show them how the entertainment system works. The best professional chauffeurs carry music and DVDs with them and offer them to passengers to enjoy for the evening. You don't necessarily have to buy a DVD or iPod and put it in the vehicle. Some companies supply them, but there are also creative ways to get them. Music companies send music videos to stereo shops to run in their showrooms; it never hurts to stop at your local shop and ask them for a copy.

The best night-out chauffeur I know carries a special briefcase for these trips. It contains everything imaginable that passengers may ask for, including cocktail napkins, drink stirrers, bottle openers, concert DVDs, movies, and CDs of various kinds of music and performers. He is also the most requested chauffeur for nights out.

Privacy, Please: Once you have shown passengers how to use the amenities in the vehicle, return to the front seat and put the partition in the up position if your vehicle is so equipped. This way you are setting the tone of privacy for the passengers. You are not there to party or join in on the conversation. You are there to safely carry them through their evening.

Meeting Point: Once you deliver your passengers to their entertainment or dining destination, establish where you will meet your passengers when they are finished at this location. Know their cell number and they know yours and you establish an approximate time and meeting place after the event. Concerts and games get crazy as they end, so it is absolutely essential that you plan on a meeting place and estimated time.

Their Stuff: It is also a good idea to keep track of any belongings your passengers wish to leave in the vehicle while they are inside their destination. As you disembark them, glance inside the vehicle and make a mental note of what is there. Always offer to put valuables like purses, cell phones, etc. in the trunk for safekeeping. This lets your passengers know that you are aware their items are in the vehicle and you want to keep them safe.

If they decide to leave them inside the vehicle, as you are re-staging the vehicle and cleaning the interior to make it ready for them again, place their valuables in a safe visible location like on the rear shelf behind the rear seat. This way when they get back in the vehicle, the items won't accidentally end up in the cracks or under the seats where they can be forgotten.

Pick-up: If your clients' destination is a fine dining establishment and they plan on a leisurely dinner, assure them that you will be in the immediate area at all times and if they give you a five or ten-minute warning call, you will pull up as close as possible to the entrance of the restaurant.

Things to Master from Chapter Eight:

- Learn what corporate travelers expect and appreciate.
- Learn your company's affiliate / network passenger policies.
- Learn how to serve leisure passengers (big tippers).
- They won't remember you getting there on time—they expect it.
- Remember: It's the "little things" that clients appreciate.

CHAPTER NINE

Special Events

The chauffeur I introduced you to at the end of Chapter 4, Robin, was a master at making passengers feel special. When he was given a night out or special celebration (birthday or anniversary) assignment, he would call the passengers before the trip and ask them if they wanted special amenities or decorations.

One Saturday I saw Robin at the garage two hours early for a night out assignment, hovering around a white stretch Lincoln limousine. When I looked inside the vehicle, I saw a "Happy Birthday" sign with red and white balloons. The bar was loaded with Diet Coke and he had plastic dishes of nuts, mints, and goldfish crackers ready.

"Well, it's Debbie's birthday," he told me when I asked him why he had made such an effort.

"Who is Debbie?" I asked. He told me that nine years prior, he had been given a driving assignment for a night out. He called the passenger before the trip and asked them if she would like anything special in the limousine. The passenger confirmed it was a birthday celebration, so Robin bought a birthday card and balloons and presented them to Debbie at her front door. Every year after, Robin was an integral part of their birthday celebration.

I am not saying a chauffeur should or has to decorate the inside of every limousine for every occasion. But nine years prior, Robin found out what the clients were celebrating and made them feel extra special. This is why they continued to hire Robin every year and why they used limousines every year for birthdays and anniversaries as a tradition. Robin figured that the first card and balloons cost him $5. He has earned several thousand dollars from this one client annually by impressing them the first time.

When you are chosen to chauffeur a prom, wedding, or another special event, you have a special opportunity. These events are life markers that people will remember for a lifetime. You can make these events even more special and memorable for your guests by doing everything you can to keep them safe, comfortable, and pampered.

Prom and Other Events with Underage Passengers

Many livery company operators view underage passengers as problematic and shy away from providing service to them. I know some companies that double their prices around prom season and even some chauffeurs who roll their eyes when they get a driving assignment for younger passengers. That is a damaging perspective. Many calls we get for proms, formals etc. come from the children of corporate clients. If we don't serve their needs, someone else will be glad to, and that may put all business with that client in jeopardy. At the very least, operators that focus solely on corporate transportation should have local affiliates they can use for their corporate clients' children. Why open the door for another company to take away your existing business? From a professional chauffeur's standpoint, driving children for affluent families is an opportunity to shine and generate additional gratuity.

Special Rules for Minors

There is one rule above all others when dealing with children: speak directly to their parents concerning the trip. It most states, it is illegal for children to enter into a contract, and reserving a chauffeur and a vehicle is entering into a contract. From a performance and liability standpoint, you must confirm everything with adults. The adult must pay the bill, and the adult must sign off on the reservation and trip sheet. It is up to the company to make sure an adult handles the trip "contract," and it is up to the chauffeur to make sure the adult is available to communicate with before, during, and after the actual event.

Many livery companies have what is called a "prom pledge" that spells out conduct that is not allowed inside their vehicles. I would extend that prom pledge to be a code of conduct that must be followed on any trip where minors are in the vehicle without adult supervision during the trip. The most important rule is no consumption or possession of alcohol or drugs in the vehicle. It is critical that the chauffeur, the adults, and the underage passengers are absolutely in agreement with this policy for this trip. Unfortunately, we are in the days of 1-800 HIRE A LAWYER, so this is something your company or you as a professional chauffeur cannot compromise on.

Before the trip, I recommend calling the parents and going through every detail of the trip. Write down any approved stops along the way. Meet parents at the initial pick-up points and give them your cell number, in case they have questions. Get a list of all the passengers who will be in the vehicle and a phone number for a parent of each of them that could be called in the event of an emergency.

It is the chauffeur's job to make sure every passenger who gets in the vehicle at the beginning of the evening returns home safely at the end of the evening. This means introducing yourself to every passenger by name and letting them know they need to tell you if they want to change plans and not return home with the group later that night. If Mary Smith does not come out of the prom or decides to run off with her boyfriend, the chauffeur needs to call Mary's parents and alert them.

All the Rest

Other than checking in with parents, agreeing on a complete itinerary, having a complete roster of passengers with full names, parent name and their phone number, these driving assignments can be treated the same as those with all adults in the vehicle. It's simple: don't treat these passengers differently than your adult passengers. Make sure you pamper them the same way and refer to them in a formal fashion. Go through your normal protocol, from familiarizing them with amenities to offering to store valuables in your trunk.

Obtain phone numbers of all the passengers who are carrying cell phones and let all of them know where you will be when they come out at the end of the prom. Never expect a group of 12 kids to stick together inside the prom or all come out together at the same time, so make sure you know who every passenger is, have their full name and cell number to call them if they turn up missing at the end of the prom.

Communicating During Prom

I used to check in with the teachers or school personnel running the event. Many times, they will be out front at arrival time. A professional chauffeur always takes this time to introduce herself and her company to school staff, who could be future customers or in the position to recommend you to other students or faculty.

I always communicate with the parents throughout the evening and ask them if they will be staying up until you return their children home. Most will tell you they are, and most appreciate you calling once at the beginning of the evening to let them know you have delivered the children to the prom and you are standing by out front.

Never leave the area under any circumstances. In most prom situations, the schools will not let the children leave the prom until the very end. However, you must plan for any emergency if one of your passengers gets hurt or sick or has to leave early. In these cases, always call the passenger's parents and notify them.

What happens when……

The passengers want to stay out an extra hour	Call their parents and your office
The passengers want you to buy them beer for an extra tip	Refuse
One of the passengers wants to go home with someone else	Call their parent for approval before you let them go
A fight breaks out in the vehicle or the passengers are being rowdy	Pull over in a safe location. Call your office, their parents, or the police if they won't settle down. Never put yourself in the middle, and never get physical or touch any of your passengers, even if they touch you.
A parent wants to load up your limousine with alcohol for the trip	I have had this happen in the past a few times. Just because the parent wants to be cool, it is not cool for them to put a cooler with a case of beer in the limousine and say, "Have a nice night, kids!" It is still illegal. What if the parent wants to come along with the children and the beer and act as bartender? It is still illegal, and you could be considered an accomplice to providing a minor with alcohol (which is known as endangering a minor or contributing to the delinquency of a minor, should law enforcement be alerted).

Be sure that the passengers are not doing anything in the vehicle that is dangerous or illegal and that you, as their "guardian by default" as I like to say, keep them safe at all times. When in doubt, call a parent or your office.

Parents will appreciate your diligence and your looking after their children and all the other children in the vehicle. If you approach the driving assignment professionally and do all the things I have advised, a handsome gratuity will be forthcoming from the parents at the conclusion of the evening.

The Wedding Chauffeur: The Couple's Concierge

Some of the best times I can remember as a professional chauffeur were while I was providing transportation service for weddings. When I started my company, I was the primary chauffeur for the first 50 weddings and loved every minute of it. I did that so I could literally handle all the details and observe everything that happened and write it all down in a training manual. Over the years, I have met hundreds of couples and helped them choose the vehicles and design the service that best suited them.

Wedding transportation is all about timing and logistics; very rarely is getting the passenger to the location on time more important. Big or small, weddings take specific timing and logistics and a focus on the smallest details. When you receive a wedding assignment, it more than likely will have special instructions and maybe even a few stops.

Planning

Weddings are usually planned months in advance, so the reservations for weddings are normally not entered on a last-minute basis. There is no excuse for lack of details on your assignments. Many companies have dedicated reservations staff to handle weddings, because it is indeed a specialized reservation and it takes a bit of time to design the timeline with the bride, whether by phone or in person.

Whether your company has a dedicated wedding sales staff or not, I always suggest that you contact the couple, wedding planner, or whoever made the reservations several days before the wedding. Introduce yourself, let them know that you are there to help, and ask if you could take a few minutes and go over the fine points of the transportation schedule. Make sure you outline the timeline clearly. Always end the call by giving out your cell phone number and letting the contact person know that she can contact you any time. You are not just a chauffeur for the wedding; you are her concierge for the day and should thus help her with anything she needs.

Special wedding supplies for your vehicle:

1) Extra vehicle cleaning supplies
2) Garment spot remover
3) Sewing kit
4) Bandages
5) Bobby pins and safety pins
6) Scotch tape
7) Extra umbrellas—enough for everyone in the wedding party
8) Cloth napkins
9) Extra men's handkerchief
10) Extra spring water (still or sparkling)
11) Cocktail napkins
12) Silver tray
13) Red carpet
14) White gloves

You may never need the things on this list but I guarantee the first time you leave one of them at home, you will be asked for it.

When I performed wedding duty, I always wore a tuxedo and white gloves to add an air of elegance and formality to what I was doing. You would be surprised how little used tuxedoes cost, and white gloves are available at any chain pharmacy. There are several things that connote luxury, refined service, and true elegance: white gloves and red carpets are two.

Traditional Wedding Transportation

Wedding transportation typically fits in to one of two categories: traditional or contemporary. Years ago, weddings were planned 18 months in advance and there were an average of 180 guests. Traditionally the parents of the bride paid for the wedding, and the groom never saw the bride in her wedding dress before the ceremony. It was considered bad luck.

Traditional transportation calls for the bride and whoever is going to walk her down the aisle and perhaps her maid of honor to ride to the ceremony location in a separate vehicle from everyone else. They usually arrive at the church just in time to walk down the aisle. In this case, the groom and the rest of the wedding party are either in another limousine or they get to the church on their own.

Immediately after the ceremony, traditional wedding transportation service calls for the bride and groom to travel to the reception site or to another site for photography, taking their first ride as man and wife completely by themselves. There may be another limousine behind them for the rest of the wedding party, including the maid of honor, bridesmaids, best man, and groomsmen. At the close of the reception, it is tradition for the bride and groom exit with fanfare into a limousine and be whisked off to their honeymoon or nearby hotel.

Contemporary Wedding Transportation

Many weddings are now planned less than a year from the wedding date, the average number of guests has dropped to about 120. The bride and groom may plan and pay for the entire event. These changes have also seen variations in the transportation provided at weddings also.

In recent years, wedding transportation has taken on a more casual, even party mode I call "contemporary." It seems to have coincided with the emergence in of the ultra stretch limousine, based on large SUV's that can carry 12, 15, or even 20 passengers. Today many brides travel to their wedding with their maid of honor, all their bridesmaids, and perhaps whoever is walking her down the aisle in a large stretch limousine. After the ceremony, the happy couple and the entire wedding party pile into the limousine and head to the reception.

Wedding Transportation Sequence

The last thing you want to do is treat a wedding like any other job. Weddings have a very specific order. Calculating how long it takes to get the various parties to the church determines pick-up times. Once at the church, the length of the ceremony and the photo shoot come in to play. Knowing the sequence of events is critical to your success.

Example of the Sequence of Wedding Transportation:

a) Groom Pick-up: deliver to the church 1 hour prior to the ceremony

b) Bride Pick-up: deliver to the church 15 minutes prior to the ceremony

c) Stand by at the church: Ceremony 25 min, photography 30-45 min

d) Drive bride and groom to the reception

e) Stand by at the reception: 3 to 4 hours

f) End of reception: drive bride and groom to their hotel

On the day of the event, the best chauffeurs I know arrive at the first pick-up location 30 minutes prior to the pick-up time. This is usually the bride's mother's house or the maid of honor's house, where all the ladies are getting ready. Introduce yourself to the important parties at this location and congratulate the parents of the bride. Tell the bride and her maid of honor how lovely they look.

As soon as you introduce yourself, talk to whoever is in charge of the logistics for the wedding. This could be a wedding planner, the mother of the bride, or the bride herself. Once you identify who is in charge, do a quick rundown of the sequence of events to make sure there have not been any changes. Then locate the photographer, introduce yourself, and map out exactly where the bride, groom, and wedding party will need to be for photography.

Once you are completely clear on what is to take place, ask if there is anything they need or anything you can carry to the car. There are usually bags to be carried to the car from the bride and her maid of honor; ask for them before they bring it up.

Beverages

Many limousine companies provide champagne, sparkling water, or other soft drinks for the bridal party. I always brought extra water and asked the person in charge if I should serve beverages at the prep location. Many times, people are waiting for the bride, and they are nervous. Offering them water is a nice gesture.

There is also a lot of waiting right after the ceremony outside the church or at a park, when the photographer starts posing the wedding party. I created what I called "silver tray service," where I walked around with either spring water or glasses of champagne and napkins on a large silver tray for the wedding party. I also carried cloth napkins and offered them to anyone who was perspiring so that sweat would not be visible in the photographs. These extra touches gave us great reviews for wedding service.

Keeping the bride, groom, and wedding party hydrated and free of perspiration for photographs is crucial. Sometimes photographers forget there is a hot sun and a timeline for the event. They may get carried away with backdrops and poses. It is your job to gently remind them to stay on schedule and keep everyone comfortable during the process.

It is also customary to have a bottle of champagne in the vehicle for the bride and groom to have their first toast as a married couple as soon as they get in the vehicle after the ceremony. I usually have the bottle open in an ice bucket wrapped in a white cloth (to avoid drips on gowns and tuxedoes). I open it in advance away from the vehicle because I do not want to see cracked vehicle glass due to an errant cork.

White Glove Service and Rolling Out the Red Carpet

Whenever I offered spring water, cocktail napkins, or cloth napkins to members of the bridal party, it was always with white gloves and a silver tray. Whenever I assisted the bride with the train of her dress, it was with clean white gloves. This just adds something to your service that is unexpected.

I am a huge fan of using a red carpet for wedding service, specifically right after the ceremony, when they exit the vehicle at the beginning of the reception, and again if they are being picked up at the end of the evening. Some companies use a red carpet for the entire event regardless of who is getting in and out of the vehicle. I always reserved this privilege for the happy couple.

Sit and Swivel

Women wear gowns for almost every wedding. Part of your job as the chauffeur is to assist women getting in and out of the vehicle and making certain nothing soils their dress. I always cleaned all the door-jambs of the vehicle right before the wedding so there wouldn't be a problem if a dress ran across it.

As ladies attempt to get in your vehicle, they will most likely pause awkwardly while trying to figure out how to do it. I recommend offering your gloved hand to assist them and say, "sit and swivel." They should sit on the seat near the door and swivel their legs in after. You can also offer to help them with the bottom of their dress when they swivel into the vehicle. This is especially important with the bride, because her dress is usually the longest. The bride is usually the last person who gets into a vehicle and the last person out of the vehicle, so prompt the seating and orchestrating the exit that way.

Adjusting the Bride's Train

The train of a wedding gown is the long part on the back that drops to the floor. The train must not get caught on anything in the vehicle. Hold it up for the bride as she enters and exists the vehicle. Traditionally the maid of honor and mother of the bride may help with this, but don't hesitate to offer your assistance, especially when the bride is entering or exiting the vehicle.

Normally the maid of honor and mother of the bride are already seated when the ceremony is about to start. Offer to adjust the bride's train right before she walks down the aisle.

Requests from the Wedding Party or Guests

On occasion, a member of the wedding party may ask you to do something. I recommend you check with the person in charge before deviating from your itinerary. The request will likely be approved, but it is important that the person who hired you knows where you are and what you are doing.

The Close

Regardless of whether the reservation ends at the reception or a hotel, it is customary to say goodbye to several people before you depart.

The Wedding Planner: If there is a wedding planner for the event, always check out with them and ask them if there is anything else they need before you leave. Let them know you are finished and make sure they are not expecting anything else. Give the wedding planner your business card as well. I can't tell you the number of times I have done this only to hear the planner say, "What about…at the end of the night?" Either the planner forgot, or the reservationist forgot to tell you about something extra. If you always say goodbye to the wedding planner and reiterate that you are finished, you may avert a disaster.

Parents: The next people to say goodbye to are the newlyweds' parents. Offer them congratulations again and tell them your part in the event is finished. I always offer them a business card and let them know that they can call us if they need anything else. This is a very professional way to make sure they are satisfied with everything and secure their business in the future. Don't be surprised if a parent lays an extra tip on you.

Newlyweds: If the last time you will see the newlyweds is when you drop them off at the beginning of their reception, say a quiet goodbye as you disembark them. Wish them luck and hand one of them a business card. Let them know you have finished your part of the evening but if they need anything, they can call your company. Add that it has been your pleasure being part of their day.

If you will be taking the newlyweds to their hotel after the reception, remind them of that and ask if they would like you to pick up anything for the ride to the hotel. When that time comes, you should go to the entrance to the reception and wait until the happy couple is ready to leave. Always ask the couple if you can carry or store their bags in your vehicle to help facilitate their exit from the reception.

One of the niceties that I developed over the years was giving couple a wedding card at the end of the evening signed by me with the title "Your Wedding Chauffeur," with a note in the card that wished them congratulations and let them know I would be honored to drive them next year for their anniversary. You would be surprised the repeat business I developed by doing that, not only from the couples themselves, but other young couples they referred.

Making Memories

There are a variety of other special events you may be asked to chauffeur: anniversaries, bar mitzvahs, Sweet 16s, reunions—the list goes on and on. Whether you are adjusting the bride's train or dropping a young couple off at prom, remember that your guests will treasure these moments for years to come. You want your guests to fondly remember how accommodating and helpful you were–and perhaps refer you to the next prom group or engaged couple who comes along.

Things to Master from Chapter Nine:

- Learn your company's prom passenger rules
- Create a repartee with parents and be sure you have their contact phone numbers
- Learn your company's rules for serving minors
- Learn how to be the best wedding chauffeur you can be

CHAPTER TEN

Celebrities

In the chauffeured transportation industry, we try to make every single passenger feel like a celebrity. However, there *are* passengers who are actually celebrities. A celebrity does not have to be a Hollywood actor or a Top 40 pop star: it is anyone recognizable by the public.

I have personally driven senators, ambassadors, presidential candidates, top musicians, stage performers, A-List actors, television stars, and sports celebrities. I have been part of parades and motorcades. I have waited at movie productions and stage performances. I have awakened celebrities in the morning and put their children to bed in the evening; I have picked up meals, beverages, and even diapers per special requests. I have shopped with them and for them and staged outside their domicile for 12-to-18-hour shifts on standby in case they decided to go for a ride in the middle of the night.

No one really trained me on how to deal with celebrities. My previous business career dealing with big egos helped, I guess. I eased into it gradually through referrals by customers who grew to trust me. As my transportation company grew, we got more and more of these high-profile assignments. I spent many enjoyable days with celebrity passengers over the years, where it was truly an honor and pleasure to serve. I also ran into one or two that were not as pleasant, but I still provided the best service available.

When I started driving less, I trusted only my best, most detail-oriented chauffeurs on these assignments. As recently as a month before I sold my company, I was requested by several celebrities. I always put on my "dress black uniform" to drive them personally. I could have risked the relationship and begged off the assignments, but I viewed it as a chance to keep my skills sharp and take a break from boring in-office duties.

Celebrities: They Aren't Just Like Us

Some chauffeurs will tell you that celebrities are "just like us." While they are mortal and indeed dress in the same garments as the rest of humanity, the last thing celebrities want is to be treated "just like us." They require special care, treatment, communication, and safeguards. If you approach driving a celebrity as "just another trip," you most likely will fail. Your company will get a black eye and never be requested by that client again.

Driving celebrity clients can be challenging and stressful, but these assignments come with great rewards and lasting (and confidential) memories. It takes special traits and more than a few of these high-profile assignments to hone the necessary skills.

Preparation

When you get one of these assignments, you must not leave anything to chance. We never received reservations from the celebrity themselves; people in these positions don't usually pick up the phone to book a ride. We got these assignments from managers, booking agents, personal assistants, or hotel or venue staff. This sometimes added to the challenge of getting all the details.

Celebrity visits can last for days and include many stops. If I had any questions, I usually asked the reservations or dispatch staff at my office if I could call the contact person directly to go over the details for the trip. I took detailed notes and repeated them back to the person. I always attached the notes to the trip sheet for the job, so I could check them with the passenger or their representative during the greeting.

Preparing the Vehicle: Ask if they require anything special in the vehicle, like specific beverages, mints, gum, or snacks. They might need wi-fi, phone chargers, 110-volt outlets, or other special equipment. I usually ask the person booking, "Does Ms. X require anything special to eat or drink, or a car equipped with wi-fi or other special equipment?" You may also wish to find out how much luggage to expect. Normally the person booking the transportation knows all these details and will volunteer them to you before you even broach the subject.

Planning Pick-ups and Drop-offs: Picking up or dropping off celebrities in public places, such as the airport, a restaurant, or a hotel, is stressful. A recognizable celebrity can draw a spontaneous crowd in seconds. Sometimes you will be asked to bring them to a service entrance, loading dock, back entrance, or specific gate or VIP entrance area. When you first converse with the person booking the transportation, it is a good idea to ask if specific arrangements have been made in this regard. You can also ask staff at your company whether this has been done or should be considered.

If you are speaking to a manager, agent, or executive assistant, ask them about specific arrangements to drop off or pick up the celebrity in non-public areas. Ask if there are any specific security arrangements that have been or need to be made. I always ask how they usually deal with photographers or autograph-seekers at this same time. Usually at that point the assistant will voice any concerns or establish any procedures for you to be aware of regarding these issues.

Mapping the Route: If I am given prior notice of a few days that I will be driving a celebrity, I drive the route, stop at every destination, and talk with the staff. I usually let airport police know, and I sometimes ask to be escorted to the gate. Acquainting yourself with all the particulars of each venue prevents issues.

Pseudonyms and Anonymity: Many celebrities travel under assumed names. Always refer to your passengers using their pseudonym. If they are traveling using their own name, when asking at hotels for them or calling on the phone, use their name discreetly so as not to draw attention.

You must keep all the details confidential. Don't tell office employees and other chauffeurs at the company, especially anyone you may encounter out in public. Never confirm or deny whom you are driving to anyone other than your supervisor or staff directly involved in the trip.

Scheduling

If their assistant is coordinating things by phone, communicate with her every step of the trip. Make it a habit of updating her at the close of each day and asking if there is anything else you should prepare for or bring with you for your next part of the assignment. Thank the person you are communicating with, whether it is the assistant or the celebrity himself, every day and asking if there is anything else he needs that evening or the next day.

A celebrity visit may last several days. Sometimes the itinerary is communicated on daily basis. At the conclusion of every day, ask for details about the following day. You may end up only getting your arrival time for the next morning, but at least you asked.

Celebrity passengers usually have very hectic schedules. Even an itinerary that is planned well in advance could change in an instant. For these assignments we add another A to your list: Adaptability. If your passenger decides that instead of going back to their hotel he wants to go to the casino and play poker for a few hours, your job is to say "Absolutely" and discreetly call or text your office to let them know the change in plans. Do not hesitate to say yes to these clients, but always notify your office of any variations to the itinerary.

Communication

When you meet the VIP, it is very important that you keep a high degree of formality and discuss only the facts necessary to accomplish your assignment. Resist the urge to discuss their career or notoriety. Under no circumstances are you to ask for a picture or autograph. If the celebrity offers for some reason, you must politely refuse and tell them it is against company policy. It is unprofessional to mention their career or that you are a big fan. Focus on a warm welcome, formal dialogue, and driving.

If the celebrity is traveling with other people, identify who they are without asking. If the celebrity is traveling with an assistant, he will usually identify himself and do all the communicating. If this happens, don't speak to the celebrity after you introduce yourself.

Special Requests

On these assignments specifically, your notebook of restaurants, cinemas, and shopping locations will come in handy. A VIP is the VERY last person in the world who wants to hear the phrase "I don't know." Early in my career, when I was still behind the wheel every day, I picked up a television personality from the airport at 9:45 p.m. I was supposed to drive her to her hotel and carry her bags to her room. At the airport I got permission to meet her right at the gate with an airport police officer (easily done for a celebrity, even now). The second she got off the plane, I introduced myself. She said, "Hi, I am dying for a chocolate soufflé."

Note: this is Tampa, Florida at 9:45 p.m. on a weeknight. This is not New York City; Tampa actually does sleep.

"As we are walking to the car I will check on that immediately for you," I said. I texted the woman who worked at the front desk of the celebrity's hotel, who I knew from my work as a chauffeur. I asked her if she knew where I could get a chocolate soufflé and included the word HELP at the end of the text. Soon, a message appeared on my phone.

"ROY'S on Boyscout but HURRY the kitchen closes at 10pm."

I discreetly called Roy's identified myself and told them I had a very important client who wanted chocolate soufflé. They told me to come right over.

Relieved, I let my passenger know I had arranged for us to pick up a chocolate soufflé on our way to the hotel. I asked if she wanted to eat it at the restaurant, which was empty to accommodate her, or if she wanted to eat it at her hotel. She was more than thrilled and chose to take it with her. That night, I found out what chocolate soufflé tasted like because the chef made two, and my passenger insisted that I take one home and have it that night, along with a handsome tip.

You are expected to know everything about the territory you are driving in, including where to find everything. That includes a one-hour dry cleaner, an all-night bait shop, and everything in between. Always answering in the affirmative is a sure way to increase your reward for a job well done at the end of the assignment.

Picking Up and Dropping Off

Some celebrities enjoy interacting with the public at chance meetings. Others absolutely do not. I have been with both types in my career, and some switch between personas on a daily if not hourly basis, so you have to be on your toes.

One day I was driving an A-list movie star with his son and friends on a day-long trip in Tampa. When I finally dropped them off at their hotel for the evening, he asked me if I knew a great restaurant for spaghetti and meatballs because that was what his young son and friends wanted for dinner.

"Yes, of course," I replied. "Would you like take out or to eat at the restaurant?"

He asked me to make reservations for that night and give them a couple hours to rest and freshen up before I came back and get them and take them to this restaurant.

I knew that if I took my VIP through the front door of the restaurant, he would be recognized in seconds. He would have had no privacy and a miserable time trying to eat with his son and friends. And so, when I left, I went directly to the restaurant and asked for the manager. When he appeared, I took him aside discreetly and told him who I was and that I was driving a very recognizable celebrity. I asked if they could accommodate a party of six on a very confidential basis in a very quiet area of the restaurant. He showed me a private room that happened to have a separate entrance (actually a fire door) for us to use. I thoroughly checked the room and mapped out a route to and from the vehicle. I then returned to the hotel and picked up my group, brought them to the restaurant, and escorted them in the fire exit door with no fanfare.

When I returned to get them in a couple hours, we left by the fire exit and I returned them to the hotel. My VIP thanked me profusely.

"The food was excellent," he told me. "This was the most peaceful meal I have enjoyed at a restaurant with my son in a very long time."

If you are not resourceful and not willing to go the extra mile, don't accept celebrity clients. Everything you do must protect the person's privacy and safety. If you are in doubt about any request, call your supervisor for assistance with last-minute or special requirements.

Sometimes you will have to discharge or pick up your celebrity guest in public view. It helps to have a plan of action to minimize gawkers or autograph-seekers.

Hotel Pick-up and Drop-off

Most hotels go to great lengths to accommodate celebrities in these situations. It always helps if you have introduced yourself to the hotel desk, concierge and management staff as the person who will be driving their "special guest." This is where aliases and pseudonyms come in handy.

If I am picking up a celebrity at a hotel, I usually ask if she would like to stay in her room until I arrive. I also suggest that she use the service elevator to get to the lobby. If the VIP has no issue with the public, he/she will usually let you know right then. If this happens, try and station your vehicle as close as you can to the entrance to the hotel. Pack all luggage before you bring down your passengers and exit as quickly as you can.

I volunteer to bring up hotel staff with a bill or return room keys so the celebrity does not have to do this personally. Usually if the celebrity is traveling with an assistant, that person handles these details, and you take your direction from him.

Security

Remember, you are not an armed security guard. You are there to provide flawless transportation and seamless logistics. However, you are there to make sure you passengers are not bothered by fans or photographers. If you think you need assistance, call your office. In almost all cases, if a celebrity is concerned about his security, he will travel with his own security personnel.

If there is no security, always position yourself between the celebrity and the public. Keep your passenger safe and at arm's length (at a minimum) from anyone he does not know. Be aware of all your surroundings, take direction from the celebrity, and gauge his reactions. You might be able to tell if he is getting anxious. If you have doubts, ask: "Sir, are you all right with this situation? If you are uncomfortable in any way, please let me know."

I have been in situations when I had to place myself between the celebrity and a moving crowd and guide the VIP by the arm to the vehicle. I locked the door right behind her, dove into the driver's seat, and took off. Your best judgment, attention to detail, and communication with your passenger are the best tools you have in these situations.

Things to Master from Chapter Ten:

- Celebrities are NOT Just like us
- Learn special preparations and protocols
- Always keep it confidential
- Don't try and become their friend
- Never take photos of them or with them

CHAPTER ELEVEN

Become an Ambassador of Your Brand

One of the biggest problems I see in the chauffeured transportation industry is what I call the "mercenary" chauffeur. Mercenary chauffeurs have a "what's in it for me" attitude. Mercenary chauffeurs usually don't smile or seem happy. Their appearance is normally disheveled, or at least not crisp, and their attitude is typically more on the negative side than the positive. When prompted, they will likely speak poorly about their company (its management and its owners), and sometimes they don't even have to be asked in order to badmouth the organization they work for.

In the office or among other chauffeurs, they seem perpetually unhappy, are always complaining, and they come off as not caring about anything but themselves and their income. These drivers are usually not customer-focused; they view all passengers as the same, or at most they put passengers in two categories: tippers and non-tippers.

This is a not just an issue in chauffeured transportation; this is a problem in the entire service sector. It is the phenomenon where workers go about their jobs expending the minimal amount of effort, with no pride in what they do, no real concern for the customer, and thinking only in terms of their weekly paycheck with no loyalty to their company, colleagues, or customers. Today the average person holds nine different jobs before they turn 60. In fact, studies show in our society typical employees are not identifying with their organization. In a survey by the Conference Board, more than 30% of all workers admit they are just showing up to collect a paycheck. The company must continually recruit because workers are more transient, customer experience suffers, mediocre service becomes the norm, and workers move from job to job—so no one wins.

Is this growing phenomenon in service industries because jobs have changed, or is it because workers' attitudes and performance have gotten worse, and thus good companies cannot survive and maintain acceptable profit margins?

This may ultimately be a chicken or egg proposition, but I submit to every worker in the service industry in the US today that if you like being the ultimate provider of a service your company delivers, you must always exceed customers' expectations, and if you do this consistently, your income will always grow year over year, and you will never be unemployed.

Can the Problem Be Solved?

Now in this book there is no way I am going to attempt to solve all the ills of jobs in the service sector, nor can I definitively answer why there are so many mediocre employees and companies out there—I am not qualified to do that; I think I would need a psychology degree. What I can and hope to do is convince people why they should be "company men and women." I hope I can convince you that being an "ambassador for your brand" will provide you with tangible rewards.

I have been a customer of chauffeured transportation for over 25 years, and I have ridden in the back passenger seat more times than I can recall. I have organized and ordered transportation for hundreds of executives and groups in my corporate and security career and have personally driven thousands of people.

I know one thing for sure about the chauffeured transportation industry:

Being a professional chauffeur is not as easy as it looks.

But in this hard business made up of many people and businesses providing barely adequate or OK service, there is a tremendous opportunity for people who care and want to excel at their career in the service of others. I can tell you definitively that the top 10% of professional chauffeurs in the luxury transportation industry earn a very comfortable living with not only very nice W-2 or 1099 income from their company, but also significant income of cash from passengers they serve well.

BECOMING AN AMBASSADOR FOR YOUR BRAND: START WITH A GOOD COMPANY

Identifying good companies to work for is easy. First and foremost, they have the best reputations in the area among their customers. Secondly, they have chauffeurs who have been with them long term and speak well of their company. Finally, their fleet is usually the most impeccably clean and best maintained in the territory. Their fleet vehicles never have dents on them, never have bald tires or scratched-up bumpers. If any of these things happen to their vehicles on the road, the best-operated companies take the vehicle out of service and address the issue quickly, usually in a matter of hours or days.

Notice I didn't identify the largest companies or largest fleets necessarily as the best companies in a market. Some large regional companies I know, even national companies, do not rate with the title "good company" for many reasons. Do your research, ask around, visit their facility, and ask questions of their customers and chauffeurs on your own.

Identifying bad companies is actually even easier than identifying good companies. They lose customers or at least fail to have lots of repeat customers and often compete via low prices. It seems they always have lots of new chauffeurs and very few veteran chauffeurs—they churn and burn personnel, as we say. The chauffeurs they have are not the cleanest or best dressed in the market. Finally, their fleet spends a lot of time parked, their vehicles are not cared for that well, and they cut corners on detailing and maintenance.

How would you know these things as someone not employed by the company? Easy: Read their online reviews on Google and sites like Trip Advisor and Yelp. Visit the company, pick up an application for employment, and ask who their veteran chauffeur is. When you get serious about working for the company, ask to meet them as part of your interview process. When you interview, ask to see the fleet, see the detail/cleaning area and look for dents or bad scratches that look like they are aged. A surefire place to look is the trunk and trunk deck: If the company cares about its fleet, it will have guards on the trunk deck or a luggage protector attached on the inside of the trunk (basically a cloth that flips out when the trunk is open and covers the bumper so luggage won't scratch it).

When I owned my first transportation company, I used to see a competitor's stretch 10-passenger Lincoln limousine around town. I could identify it in an instant, because it was missing the wheel cover that is in the center of the factory rim on the rear passenger side (near the door customers always use—hello). I saw this limousine go months and months with this cover missing. Finally, as a joke, I went on eBay and for $18.00 I bought a replacement and sent it to the competitor with my business card attached to it. He never replied or said thanks, so I don't think he got the joke, and I don't think it made a difference. His fleet is still poorly maintained, and his business has not grown. It has a revolving door of chauffeurs, every competitor in the area complains about how cheap his prices are, and no one takes affiliate work from him or gives him any of their overflow work.

Eyes and Ears of the Company

Assuming you are working for a good company, I want you to ask yourself one question: What are you doing every single day to bring more customers to this good company so it can grow and you can get more trips? Being the best possible professional chauffeur is only part of the answer. After you have read this book, I would expect you to adopt the elements and strategies discussed within to do that. But that is NOT the entire answer to my question.

Have you ever heard the phrase "A rising tide lifts all boats"? It is a phrase many politicians and economists use that refers to the "big picture" and the premise that improvements in the general economy will benefit all participants in that economy. I use it here to suggest that additional sales, additional customers, and additional improvements in your company in general will benefit all employees of your company. Unlike administrative, reservation, dispatch, and even executive staff at your company, who are stuck in the office every day, you are out and about in your market area. You should see yourself not just as a chauffeur, but as part of the eyes and ears of the company.

Being an ambassador of your brand involves:

1) Observing what's going on in your market

2) Proactively meeting people who could benefit from your services

3) Telling the company story daily

4) Reporting back to company sales, marketing, or executives on opportunities

The best brand ambassadors I know carry their company's new customer creation salesperson's business cards with them, as well as their own chauffeur business cards. They also carry company brochures or promotional material (in envelopes to keep them clean) so that when they meet a potential new customer, they have something to leave behind. It also helps greatly if you have a nametag that has your full company name on it.

Observe the Market

As you are on your driving assignments, look for new business growth like new stores, new professional offices, and new office buildings opening or new tenants moving in to them. New businesses are looking for new vendors in the area, so it never hurts to write down company names and addresses of these locations and bring them back to the office.

When you are picking up passengers in an office complex, for example, if you are very early, rather than sitting down the street listening to the radio, drive the area and write down the names and addresses of the businesses next to where you pick passengers up. If you have the time and are feeling bold, walk into the reception area of the business and introduce yourself. Try saying something like this: "I am in the neighborhood picking up a passenger (never give specific company or passenger names) and I was wondering if I could leave this information with you to pass on to the person who plans meetings or travel for your company."

I have found that no one ignores someone or is offended if a sharply dressed person who speaks well approaches them in a business situation and asks for routine information. Normally, seven out of ten people will give you the information you requested.

There is also a surefire way to gain information about new companies or potential new customers moving to your area: Read the news section and business section of all the local newspapers and business journals in your area each week, and convey this information to your company.

You don't have to cull the area or newspapers for information and barrage your company with tens and hundreds of leads each week to be an effective brand ambassador. Simply think about the passengers you drive every day, think about what they do and where they work. Consciously be on the lookout for those types of companies and people who could become new customers for your company.

Proactively Meet Prospective New Customers

Every day, every chauffeur in the country passes by people who could become new customers of the company they work for and usually never make the connection. Why? Let's keep it simple: Try meeting new customers where you pick up passengers.

At Airports

You are never supposed to openly solicit passengers at airports, so I am not directing any chauffeur to do that. What I am suggesting is that you look out for a passenger that may either need directions as they come down in to baggage claim or may possibly need help with their luggage and offering to assist them. Make sure you are displaying your company name tag and just happen to have a fresh business card in your top shirt pocket. When you are giving them directions or after you assist them to the elevator or curb with their luggage, simply proffer your business card and let them know if they ever need transportation, feel free to contact you or your company. Here is a great example of what I am talking about.

One day I landed in Boston and was out front of JetBlue waiting for my ride (who was late, by the way). I observed several chauffeurs both in baggage claim and outside near their vehicles. One particular chauffeur approached me as I walked to the traffic lane where livery services were supposed to stage to meet their passengers. He was dressed in a black raincoat with a company logo and his name below it. He asked if he could help me find my ride. I said I was waiting for Company X and he said, "There is no car from them in the line yet, but you may sit inside that heated booth while you wait."

"Thanks," I said. "I am curious—do you get paid to do this?"

"No," he answered. "I am early for picking up my client, and you looked like you needed help."

I asked him for his card. "Do you ever get new customers from this?" I said as he handed it to me.

He didn't answer the question. He just smiled. "If your ride doesn't show up, call our office; we will have a car here in 15 minutes," he said.

This guy was so personable no one would accuse him of doing anything but helping people and making a great impression.

At Hotels

When I was a chauffeur and I had a hotel pick-up, if I had time I always tried to arrive 30 minutes prior and work the outside driveway. I made my presence known, struck up conversations with hotel employees, and let them know who I was and what we did. Between trips, I brought them cold drinks.

I suggest being a brand ambassador only at hotels where you are actually picking up guests, unless you have approval from management at your company to stop by hotels between trips. The next time you are at a hotel picking up a guest and you are a few minutes early, announce yourself at the front desk and the concierge desk. Say something like, "I'm early but I am here to pick up (Guest Name). Here is my card, just in case you see him before I do." When you approach the desk, always have your business card in hand.

At hotels where your company frequently picks up guests, take great pains to learn the names of the front desk staff, managers, concierge staff, and valets. Make sure to say hello to them, using their names, every time you pick up at the hotel. Offer your business card and cell number, and let them know you will help their guests any way you can if they have a transportation need.

I also recommend that companies give all hospitality and lodging employees discounts on non-prime-time night-out transportation and deep discounts on airport transportation. If you do this, the people who are in the position to recommend you have actually used your service before. People recommend people they know and trust as being reliable, so whenever you are at their hotel, make it a point to acknowledge them and let them know you are around and your company is doing well. If you do this every time you pick up, they will think you are the busiest chauffeur who comes to their hotel.

Know How to Sell Yourself

When I taught salespeople for a living a hundred years ago, I used to teach them to create and memorize two things to communicate to everyone they met who could be a great prospect for the services we provided.

1) a thirty-second elevator greeting
2) a two-minute commercial about themselves and the company.

The Thirty-Second Elevator Greeting

A simple one-paragraph introduction of yourself and the services your company provides that is simple and quick that you could rattle off to everyone you meet. It might sound something like this.

"Hi, my name is Ken. I am a transportation specialist from Ambassador Limousine and Sedan. We have a 60-vehicle fleet ranging from sedans, SUV's and limousines to huge motor coaches—we even have three Rolls-Royce private limousines. We provide chauffeured transportation for all life's occasions and chauffeured service to all airports." Extend your hand with a business card.

Two-Minute Commercial

This is really an expanded version of a thirty-second elevator greeting. It offers a bit more information about the company and usually ends with a sentence that suggests how the person you're speaking to could use your service.

For a Corporate Traveler at Airport: "At Ambassador Limousine, we are known for providing the best corporate transportation. All our chauffeurs have undergone rigorous background checks and are subject to strict confidentiality agreements. We provide service for major corporations in the area because our fleet is brand new, we have WiFi in most vehicles, and we have corporate coaches that are low profile on the outside with limousine amenities on the inside."

For an Existing Passenger's Neighbor: "Ambassador is the best way to get to the airport with lots of luggage. We have a fleet of SUVs that fit six people each, plus lots of luggage. We also have great ultra stretch limousines for nights out or birthday parties, concerts, or games. Here is my card; if I can be of assistance, please let me know."

I recommend giving people either a generic company card with your name on it as a point of reference, or your own business card with your cell number and the company number on it. Even if your company doesn't supply them, spending $25 for a set of cards with your name, the title "Transportation Specialist," and your cell number is a great investment in your future income.

In politics they say, "Decisions are made by those who show up." In the case of chauffeured transportation, people choose familiar brands. If every chauffeur tells the company's story every day in between trips, common sense tells us that at least a small percentage of people who have heard the story will remember us and call us or tell a friend should a need arise.

Report Back to Management Staff

Remember when I said that in today's business environment, operating a luxury transportation company is very difficult? Keep this in mind as you attempt to give information to the company you think could result in a new customer. Don't expect accolades the first day, and don't be upset if staff appears busy or maybe even unappreciative when you convey the information. Remember the business is hectic and they are most likely overwhelmed.

Pass the information in writing in a very simple format. Include:

Who

What

Where

Why am I providing this information

I also recommend asking who usually follows up on new sales information. If the answer is not clear, then I would bring the information to your direct supervisor for her to pass up the chain. I do not suggest giving it to the owner or CEO of the company yourself. I always suggest following the chain of command to avoid looking like a suck-up and avoid upsetting people between your position and the executive level.

Let your supervisor know that you are going to continue to be on the lookout for new customers and if he/she has any suggestions, you will follow them. Remember, you are attempting to increase trips for the entire company, not yourself. In order for you to succeed, the company must succeed.

BECOME A STANDOUT EMPLOYEE

Another example of being a great brand ambassador is to become the most requested chauffeur in the company. Become the chauffeur all your passengers talk about with their friends and family.

How you become the most requested? To start with, you must consistently impress every passenger with great service and by going above and beyond what they expect, and anticipating and fulfilling their needs.

Some Examples:

During Pick-up

- Retrieve the newspaper at the end of their driveway when you pull up for the pick-up.
- Ask them if they would like you to check their mailbox for them and go to the mailbox and deliver it to them on every future pick-up

- Ask them if it is close to trash day and if they want you to put out the cans
- If you know the passengers are leaving for vacation, offer to stop by their house between trips and put the mail somewhere hidden and pick up the newspapers off the driveway or move the trash barrels off the street.

During the Ride

- Carry snacks and beverage alternatives at all times, and ask passengers if they have any special requests for future trips.
- Carry fresh newspapers and magazines on different subjects and let the passenger know they can take them with them on their trip if they like. Getting these at no cost is easy; find a hotel that will let you have a copy of today's paper and call local magazines and tell them you have "hundreds of passengers every month" and you would like to stop at their offices and pick up a supply to promote the magazine.

For Night-Out Service

Call the passengers the day of the event or the night before and ask them if there is a special occasion and ask of they would like snacks or anything special in the vehicle.

For Late or Early Airport Pick-ups

- Call the night or day before and ask if they would like you to get them something to eat or drink for the ride.

True story—back when I started Ambassador Limousine, I culled through local magazines and newspapers to find out who the movers and shakers of business were in my area. I came across a guy who made infomercials, named Kevin Harrington. One day I visited his office in my black suit between trips with a fruit basket and told the receptionist I had to personally deliver this. She showed me to his assistant. I simply handed the fruit basket to her with a card that said: "I read about you recently and wish you continued success. The next time you need a ride home from the airport, please call me. I would be honored to handle it personally."

Sure enough, his office called soon. When I picked him up at the airport, I noticed that his carry-on bag had a broken handle. I asked him about it and he said it just happened on this trip.

"If you want, I'll take it to get it repaired for you," I offered. I went to the mall, got it fixed at a shoe repair shop, and brought it to his office the next day with a note thanking him for trying our services. The next thing I knew, I was his personal driver, and his company became a major client for our company. I got a $500 Christmas bonus from him that year.

Flash forward four years, when he was being recruited by a new publicly traded company. He literally said to the recruiter, "Part of my package is Ken Lucci, my driver." The recruiter said that they had a national contract with another company, "He's my driver," said Kevin. "We now use Ambassador exclusively or I don't take the job."

The rest is history. I know for a fact that he has told the story about me fixing his luggage to dozens of people. It has resulted in Ambassador being used by many people Kevin associated with in business and socialized with personally.

Cost to repair the carry-on luggage handle: **$14.00.**

A passenger choosing me as his personal driver and him retelling that story many times to people who also became loyal customers: **priceless**.

So we are near the end of this book, and if you are like me, after you read a typical book, you may be inclined to say to yourself, "That's nice; great stuff" and then put the book down someplace until you think you need it again or management decides on a retraining session and uses the book for reference.

Well, I would like to challenge that behavior and ask you NOT to put this book away. In order to be the best at anything, you need to practice new skill sets, so if you liked what you read in this publication and think the information could positively impact your income…

Things to Master from Chapter Eleven:

- Become the ambassador of your brand.
- You control your income much more than the dispatcher or company owner.
- Create a written plan of attack on what you are going to do to create an awesome service experience each time you serve a passenger (guest).

CHAPTER TWELVE

Make a Commitment to Yourself, Your Passengers and Your Company

Remember this quote from George Steinbrenner, the late owner of the New York Yankees, which I wrote earlier in this book:

> *"If you are not going to wake up every morning and strive to be the best at what you do, why even get out of bed?"*

I was truly blessed and fortunate to have known Mr. Steinbrenner well and watched him operate his businesses first hand. I listened and learned the spirit he instilled in every person who worked for him in his businesses and every player of his major league and minor league teams.

He was one of the few owners who would meet with every player individually before each season and collectively with all the coaches, managers, and support personnel. He met each one to impart his philosophy of winning in life, in business, and on the field, and how he expected members of his teams to perform.

Many times I heard him speak in many forums, and I was fascinated by one comparison he made often—the distinction between being a player and being a warrior. Here is a summary.

He would describe a very frequent play in baseball when the pitcher throws a curve ball and the batter hits a "pop fly-foul ball" and the ball heads to the foul line near third base and he described two ways outfielders approached the same play:

Outfielder #1 looks up and follows the ball in the sky, runs over to where he thinks the ball will drop, and has his glove up over his head. When he notices the ball is definitely going to go into foul territory and definitely going to drop in the stands, he drops his glove and walks back to his position in the outfield.

Outfielder #2 looks up and follows the ball in the sky and runs at full speed over to where he thinks the ball will drop with his glove up over his head. When he notices the ball is definitely going to go into foul territory, he runs faster! When he notices the ball is going to go into the stands, he jumps over the barrier, dives into the stands, catches the ball, raises his glove triumphantly in the air with the ball in it so everyone sees he caught it, gets off the spectator he fell on, brushes himself off, gives the ball to the youngest spectator in his view, and does a celebratory wave to the crowd who cheers louder than before.

Both are descriptions of good outcomes to the play, but which outfielder would you consider the warrior of the two? Obviously **Outfielder #2, right? CORRECT!**

How Can a Chauffeur Perform Like Outfielder #2?

1) He doesn't do just what is adequate to make the play (drive from A to B)

2) He pushes himself to his maximum capability to show the

Make a Commitment to Yourself, Your Passengers and Your Company

bosses he is a leader (at his craft and in his industry).

3) He pushes himself to his maximum capability every play (on every trip)

4) He impresses his teammates (fellow chauffeurs and staff)

5) He impresses the spectators (his ultimate customers)

I learned many things from watching George Steinbrenner, his sons, his executives, and his teams, and I can tell you this philosophy permeates his organization, down to the guy who picks up the trash and sweeps the floors of the stadium.

The difference between just doing what is adequate and doing the maximum you are capable of doing in my opinion is one of the big reasons why the New York Yankees are the winning-est team in the history of the sport. I coined it the *"The Mystique of the Pinstripes"*

What is my point?

I want you to make a commitment to be the best in your chosen field.

DO IT for your company—even though you may not like everything they do.

DO IT for company staff—even though you may not agree with them all the time.

DO IT for your fellow chauffeurs—even though you may think you may compete with them for trips assignments. Remember, a rising tide lifts all boats.

DO IT for your guests—so they will be exceptionally pleased with your service, recommend you and your company and tip you more.

DO IT FOR YOURSELF—BE A WARRIOR

Be an example for other chauffeurs, and be the best-paid chauffeur in your market—and you ultimately control that.

Driving Your Income

The company puts you on the field, but you control the outcome of each play.

Professional Chauffeur Performance Pledge

- I affirm that reliability, flexibility, dedication, and commitment to task are the most important qualities I must exercise to succeed in my position.
- I will arrive on time and be prepared to execute my duties professionally, expeditiously and efficiently on behalf of my company and my guests.
- I will make sure my vehicle is clean in appearance, adequately appointed, mechanically ready, and properly staged for all my driving details.
- I will operate my vehicle at all times with the utmost safety and care for the enjoyment and convenience of my guests.
- I will listen and attend to the needs of my guests with hospitality, anticipation, and diligence for as long as they are in my charge.
- I will master all the elements of Service DNA and continually improve and refine my performance.
- I will provide an exceptional customer experience to my guests in a moving environment of safety, comfort, and refinement.
- I will hold in strict confidence all I hear and observe while in the service of my company and my guests.
- I will behave with the utmost propriety while on duty and while in the possession of my vehicle, being professional and dignified at all times.
- I will be diligent in the care, operation, and handling of livery vehicles while they are in my possession.
- I will listen and take direction from staff (all variety) and my guests at all times, in order to provide an exceptional guest experience on every driving detail.
- I will act in the best interest of my guests, my fellow chauffeurs, staff, and my company at all times.
- I will maintain a positive attitude, professional appearance, and air of confidence and dignity while discharging my duties on behalf of my guests.
- Professional Chauffeur Service Values

Make a Commitment to Yourself, Your Passengers and Your Company

I Am Proud to Be a Professional Chauffeur

1) I build strong relationships and create guests for life when I perform my duties to the best of my ability every day.
2) I never take a guest for granted. I earn their business and my gratuity with every interaction.
3) I am always responsive to the expressed and unexpressed wishes and needs of my guests. The answer to every question is "Yes, of course" or "My pleasure."
4) I am empowered to create unique, memorable, and personal experiences for our guests.
5) I understand my role in the success of my company and the chauffeured transportation industry.
6) I continuously seek opportunities to innovate and improve the guest experience and my performance.
7) I own and immediately resolve guest problems and inform management after solving the problem as necessary.
8) I create an environment of teamwork and mutual support so that the needs of our guests and each employee are met.
9) I make the time and have the opportunity to continuously learn and grow.
10) I am responsible to plan the work that affects me, practicing the 7 P's.
11) I speak positively about my co-employees and our company at all times.
12) I am proud of my professional appearance, language, and conduct.
13) I protect the privacy and safety of our guests, my co-employees, and the company's confidential information and assets at all times.

14) I am responsible for providing uncompromising levels of customer service in order to ensure exceptional guest experiences on each trip.

15) I understand that our brand name is one of the most valuable assets in my charge, and I pledge that my actions and conduct will enhance its value.

16) I treat passengers as MY guests whenever I provide service and communicate with them.

17) If there is any problem that will negatively affect the guest experience, I do my best to immediately solve the issue and then inform management.

EPILOGUE

A Final Word

The current state of the chauffeured transportation industry

All over the world in every country, there are agencies of governments whether national, state, or local that make laws and regulations concerning vehicles and the passenger transportation industry. In the USA there are mammoth federal agencies involved including the US Department of transportation (USDOT), and the Environmental Protection Agency (EPA) to name just two, but there are many, many more. Federal agencies involved in vehicles, passengers and transportation:

- National Highway Traffic Safety Administration (NHTSA)
- Federal Highway Administration (FHWA)
- Federal Motor Carrier Safety Administration (FMCSA)
- United States Department of Labor
- The Internal Revenue Service (IRS)

Many States, counties and major cities have:

- Department of, or Secretary of, or Agency dedicated to Transportation
- Department of, or Secretary of, or Agency dedicated to Labor
- Department of, or Secretary of, or Agency dedicated to Consumer Affairs
- Department of, or Secretary of, or Agency for the collection of taxes
- Department of, or Agency, or special commission specifically dedicated to the taxi and chauffeured transportation business

Existing chauffeured transportation providers think of these agencies and their body of regulations one way, the public (if they know about them) thinks of them another way and "disruptors" like Uber and Lyft et al it appears think of them as irrelevant and unnecessary.

In my view, most "regulators," with some very notable exceptions, completely abdicated their responsibility when it came to allowing "booking app" providers into our industry well ahead of necessary regulations to ensure public safety was achieved as the industry evolved. Having said that, it is also my belief that governments and bureaucratic agencies ultimately correct their mistakes and in the case of chauffeured transportation will eventually achieve a balance between an open market and the need for fair regulations to protect the public, chauffeurs—and yes, business owner / operators. Whether the regulations in your area of operation that govern chauffeured transportation are in your eyes, right or wrong, fair or unfair, existent or non, rest assured of one thing: Ultimately, you as a chauffeur are responsible for the safety of your passengers—always morally, and if you are an independent operator, also legally.

A Final Word

I listed these examples to emphasize the serious laws, regulations, and rules that govern the passenger transportation business. Whether you drive passengers full or part time, please consider this advice:

1) Recognize that you are ultimately responsible for the safety of every passenger while they are in your vehicle.
2) Recognize that you have serious personal liability if something goes wrong with passengers in the vehicle and you are found to be negligent.
3) Recognize that if the vehicle you are driving is not properly insured for commercial use, you and the company you drive for face legal sanctions.
4) Make sure you possess any permit or license needed to transport passengers in commerce.
5) Make sure those permits or licenses extend to the vehicle and the company you drive for as well, and make sure they are up to date.
6) If you own the vehicle, make sure you carry commercial livery insurance on your vehicle. Consult with a commercial insurance expert, in any case.
7) Never ever overload your vehicle above the legal capacity of passengers.
8) Always require every passenger to use safety belts at all times.
9) Always wear your safety belt—you set the tone for safety.
10) If your company is doing anything illegal or asks you to do something illegal, don't drive for them.

The chauffeured transportation industry is in the vortex of a regulatory storm where many different stakeholders are arguing about regulations and laws from a variety of positions. This affects you and your passengers seriously and directly. When the dust settles, and it must, it is my belief that the regulatory environment will look much different than it does today.

What I am fearful of is that it will take a catastrophic event like numerous serious vehicle accidents with multiple fatalities involving a driver working for Uber or a similar company to advance these regulatory issues to a fair and uniform conclusion.

If that happens, all parties involved—insurance providers, regulators, technology barons, consumer advocates, public officials and lawyers—will attempt to shift the legal and moral consequences of their collective failure to protect consumers. One thing will be certain; if this occurs, the ultimate losers will be the drivers of the cars and the passengers who pay with their lives.

CPSIA information can be obtained
at www.ICGtesting.com
Printed in the USA
FFHW021649071218
49806855-54312FF

9 781478 788850